R.E.I. Editions

All of our ebooks can be read on the following devices:
- Computers
- eReaders
- iOS
- Android
- Blackberries
- Windows
- Tablet
- Cellular

Susan Daniel

Crystal Therapy

ISBN: 978-2-37297-1775

Published: November 2015
New updated edition: January 2023
Copyright © 2015 - 2023 R.E.I. Editions
www.rei-editions.com

Susan Daniel

Crystal Therapy

R.E.I. Editions

Indice

Crystal Therapy 11

Aquamarine 19

Agate 21

Alexandrite 24

Amazonite 25

Amber 27

Amethyst 29

Ametrine 31

Angelite 32

Antimonite 33

Apatite 34

Apophyllite 35

Aragonite 36

Astrophyllite 37

Atlantisite 38

Aventurine 39

Azurite 41

Biotite 42

Blenda 43

Boji Stone 44

Chalcedony 45

Yellow calcite 46

Celestine 47

Kyanite 48

Coral 49

Carnelian 50

Crysocolla 52

Jasper 53

Heliotrope 55

Hematite 56

Fluorite 57

Galena 58

Jade 59

Garnet 60

Howlite 61

Jaietto 62

Labradorite 63

Apache Tear 64

Lapis lazuli	65
Larimar	67
Magnetite	68
Malachite	70
Mookaite	71
Bull's Eye	72
Hawk's Eye	73
Cat's Eye	74
Tiger's Eye	75
White Onyx	77
Opal	78
Boulder Opal	79
Opalite	80
Obsidian	81
Sunstone	83
Moonstone	84
Pyrite	86
Citrine Quartz	87
Smoky Quartz	88
Hyaline Quartz	89

Rose Quartz 90
Rutilated Quartz 91
Tourmalinate Quartz 92
Rhodochrosite 93
Rhodonite 94
Ruby 95
Selenite 97
Seraphinite 98
Serpentine 99
Shiva Lingam 100
Shungite 101
Emerald 102
Sodalite 104
Sugillite 106
Iron Tiger 107
Topaz 108
Imperial Topaz 110
Tourmaline 111
Turquoise 112
Turchesite 114

Unakite 115
Sapphire 116
The Stones of the Zodiac 118
   Aries 121
   Taurus 123
   Gemini 125
   Cancer 127
   Leo 129
   Virgo 131
   Libra 133
   Scorpio 135
   Sagittarius 137
   Capricorn 139
   Acquarius 141
   Pisces 143

Crystal Therapy

Crystal therapy is a complementary practice that uses the energy of crystals, precious and semi-precious stones, to combat ailments of the body and mind.

There are many properties of stones, each one deserves a separate study and, if we intend to approach crystal therapy, we must know these properties, so as to choose the most suitable stone according to our needs.

Crystal therapy is based on the analysis of the chakras and provides for their treatment through the stones.

If one or more of our chakras don't "work" properly, we are affected physically and spiritually; the stones, thanks to their energies, restore balance.

From yoga philosophy crystal therapy has assimilated the concept of "chakra" which are the seven areas of our body where energy is concentrated. Stones, like plants and animals, are part of nature and would therefore be able to emit energy and vibrations and being matter in a state of perfect balance, they would be capable of transmitting positive influences.

However, it must always be kept in mind that the "stones" have no healing power of their own, so they cannot replace the work of the doctor or any drugs but, according to an oriental concept, applied to the various chakras, can only act by vibratory affinity. In crystallotherapy those areas of the human body where there are the main correspondences of the energy or reflex centers are used as therapeutic principles of application, which are also found in the study of the meridians of Acupuncture, Yoga and Ayurveda, and which are not contradiction with current scientific research.

The main thing to be able to implement crystal therapy, of course, is to have a certain basic quantity of crystals, gems, stones.

The choice of the sample is important, but even more important is that it is not an imitation, is not synthetic (artificially reproduced) and is not sophisticated (for example altered in the original colouring). Subsequently, the chosen crystals are applied to the corresponding areas or around the body, following particular patterns and procedures, depending on the type of mineral and other parameters. History testifies that the first traces relating to the therapeutic abilities of stones and crystals were found in an Egyptian papyrus dating back to 1600 BC. According to what can be read on the subject today, it seems that there were no places and peoples where stones and crystals were not used regularly for therapeutic purposes: from the ancient Egyptians to the Native Americans, from the Mayas to the Aztecs and Tolzeks, up to to the Australian aborigines, to the Celtic and Mediterranean populations.

In all these peoples, and according to traditions that have their origins in ancient times, sick people were made to wear necklaces made with various types of stones and crystals around their necks: lapis lazuli, malachite and red jasper were some of the most used and allowed the disorder and the pain of crossing them and being lost.

In addition to the ancient Egyptians, some of the original peoples of North America made continuous and methodical use of stones and crystals for various purposes. The oldest scholar who dealt in a particularly thorough way with this topic and with crystal therapy in general was the Greek philosopher Theophrastus, who lived about 400 years before Christ.

In his book of stones, in addition to reaffirming the therapeutic aspect of crystals, he underlines how it is possible to distinguish with certainty the "sex" of the stones, that is, whether they are male or female, based on the color tone; it is a very important distinctive element when crystals are used for healing purposes as the use of one of the two species greatly affects the two essential aspects of the human being: Yin (feminine) and Yang (masculine).

Many centuries later, almost at the end of the nineteenth century, John Hill, the English translator of all of Theophrastus' work, hypothesized that the therapeutic properties of stones were due in particular to the metallic minerals they contained.

Of course, modern medicine turns up its nose in the face of this type of therapy considered unscientific, but it is equally true

that shamans, medicine men, healers from all over the world have used it, and still use it, to treat people.
And with excellent results.
Stones and crystals therefore represent the tool that the healer uses to transmit the energy of the Earth and the Universe to the human being, an energy which is obviously associated with the intrinsic energy of the stone.
In humans, the energy assimilation of crystal therapies takes place through the aura and the strength centers (chakras).
The crystals and stones, arranged appropriately on the vital centers of the body (chakra) or in the nodal points of the environments, help to restore and balance the system of energies present, favoring an energy exchange that stimulates the natural healing mechanisms. The crystal, therefore acting as an energy collector, would be able to trigger the phenomenon of self-healing. The right stone should be chosen based on one's character, personality, color and also contingent situations.
Generally who is attracted:
- From the aquamarine, it is introspective and instills calm.
- Made of agate, it is communicative, practical and can give confidence to others.
- Of amber origin, it has a sweet and sensitive character, but does not yet have a well-defined personality.
- From the diamond, she loves luxury, wealth, power.
- Made of jade, he is quite practical and knows how to overcome difficult situations easily.
- From the ruby, it has a good psychophysical balance.
- From the emerald, tends to introspection and has good analytical skills.
- From turquoise, loves tranquility and calm.

Also, who has a preference for:
- White Stones, has an intuitive and creative character, but is also a dreamer and a bit lazy.
- The yellow stones, has a dynamic personality and often wants to impose his point of view on others.
- Green stones, give great importance to harmony and feelings.

- The red stones, has a strong and strong-willed character.
- Blue stones, loves serenity, is available but also a little naive. It aspires to large spaces and lofty ideals.
- Purple stones, has a calm and meditative character and is prone to introspection.
- Brown stones, has an orderly and methodical character. He fears being overwhelmed by feelings.
- Black stones, has magnetism and charm, a restless and somewhat mysterious personality.

So some general rules apply:
It is preferable to bring tumbled or polished stones.
Another rule to follow is to never wear the zodiac stone corresponding to the previous sign.
Together with the stones of your sign you should also carry the complementary stone which has the effect of mitigating the harshness and excesses of your character.

Furthermore, stones are closely linked to colors because they absorb and reflect their energies:
• Jasper, agate, ruby and carnelian, red colored stones, have the property of instilling vitality and well-being.
• Topaz, citrine and yellow stones are generally useful for overcoming shyness; in fact yellow, the color of the sun, instills confidence and energy.
• Green is the color that puts you in harmony with nature and green stones such as emerald and malachite help you find serenity.
• Blue stones, such as lapis lazuli and sodalite, stimulate intellectual activities.
• The turquoise color contains the energy of yellow and the serenity of blue and stones of this color are ideal for those suffering from anxiety and depression.
• Purple stones, especially amethyst, enhance intuitiveness. Black stones, such as onyx and obsidian, instill courage. Pink colored stones are effective for gaining more self-confidence.

Rose quartz, worn as a pendant around the neck, to touch the heart chakra, helps to give harmony to this center but all the stones of the quartz family, worn around the neck, confer wellbeing because they purify and balance the energy fields of the fourth and fifth chakra. If you want to have your stone always close to you, you can wear it set in a ring or bracelet or carry it in your bag or pocket. The important thing is that it is within our aura, that halo of light that envelops the body from birth.

Once purchased and brought home, it is important to find a container in which to store the crystals: it is better to use a container made of natural material such as, for example, glass, porcelain, ceramic or wood. Never use metal containers (unless they are noble metals such as gold or silver) or plastic.

Above all, metal should be avoided because it risks compromising the energy strength of the stones and their therapeutic and spiritual properties. If you start from the concept of using crystals on yourself or on people, it is equally important that once you get home, the stones are cleaned. There are several cleaning methods, simple and natural. First of all, they must be washed with abundant running water or, better still, they must be left to soak for at least twenty-four hours completely immersed in water, adding a small handful of fine or coarse salt.

After that, you need to remove them from the water and dry them carefully with a clean cloth that, if possible, does not release traces of fiber: in this way they are already ready to be used therapeutically.

Another way to charge stones energetically is to expose them to moonlight. It must, however, always be almost full or full and always on the rise, never on the wane.

This is because the waxing moon propagates a much stronger energy than the waning one: as far as possible, try to follow the path of this satellite, moving the stones, for example, from one window to another.

The sun is also very good, but be careful not to expose them for too long or too often, as the ultraviolet rays risk damaging them, causing them to lose their typical brilliance or original colour.

The cleaning of the crystals must therefore be done very carefully, even if the operations indicated above are sufficient for a beneficial and effective reuse even after only half a day.
Each crystal has its own crystal lattice in which the atoms occupy a well-defined place, vibrating rhythmically; in this way the atoms would transmit the vibrations of the energy present in the outermost shell where the electrons capable of displacement are. These vibrations can interact with the cells of our body restoring the altered harmony and "since the disease of the physical body is a reflection of the energetic disharmonies of the material bodies and healing occurs when their balance is restored, it is evident that it is sufficient to place the suitable crystal in the area of energetic disturbance and allow it to restore the balance to obtain the healing of all the different bodies, from the physical to the immaterial ones on which above all the action of the crystals manifests itself".
The large mineral families are essentially divided into seven large groups; each stone of these groups has different characteristics, as well as an attunement with each of the seven chakras.

1. Cubic or isometric system (diamond, garnet).
   The most common shapes are the cube and the octahedron. It is a system that has the maximum crystalline symmetry: three axes of equal length that intersect each other at right angles.

2. Hexagonal system (emerald, aquamarine).
   The most common shapes are the prism and the double pyramid. It is a system that has four axes: a main vertical axis that is longer or shorter than the other three which are equal and intersect each other at 60°.

3. Tetragonal system (zircon, rutile).
   The most common shapes are the four-sided prism and the tetragonal double pyramid. It is a system that has three axes that are all perpendicular to each other: two of

them are of equal length, while the third is longer or shorter than the others.

4. Trigonal System (quartz, sapphire).
The most common shapes are the prism and the rhombohedron. Crystals belonging to this system are sometimes regarded as crystals of the hexagonal system, as it also includes six-sided crystals.

5. Triclinic system (turquoise, sunstone).
The only common form is the pinacoid, i.e. a structure with two parallel faces. It is a system that has three axes of different lengths which intersect at angles that are never right.

6. Orthorhombic system (peridot, olivine, topaz).
The most common shapes are the rhombic prism and the pyramid with rounded ends. It is a system that has three axes which all intersect perpendicularly to each other, of different lengths.

7. Monoclinic system (jadeite, moonstone).
The most common shapes are the prism and the pinacoid. It is a system that has three axes of different lengths, two of which intersect at oblique angles and the third is perpendicular to the others.

The shape of the stone would also play an important role and some shapes would be preferred over others:
- It is believed that round stones would promote fertility.
- The square stones would be bearers of prosperity and would help to find physical well-being.
- The triangular-shaped stones and crystals, worn as lucky charms, would be protective.
- Lastly, oval-shaped stones would encourage creativity.

Furthermore, the crystals inserted in the jars of creams and oils accelerate the cell renewal process and amplify the therapeutic properties of the creams and oils themselves, improving the appearance of the skin which is relaxed and rejuvenated.

Before using crystals for this purpose it is important to purify and wash them well. They are then placed in the creams and oils, tightly closing the containers which will have to rest for at least 20 days. Later you can use them without extracting the crystals.

- For the hands and body, we place a Green Tourmaline crystal.
- In the face cream, we add a Rose Quartz and we get a bright and fresh skin.
- We add an Amethyst to the anti-acne cream with the aim of purifying the skin.
- The Hyaline Crystal is added to the cellulite cream.
- We add an Agate in the oil to massage, tone and energize the body.
- We add a Carnelian into the leg cream, to have them light and snappy, facilitating circulation.

Crystals have a beneficial effect on us, even if we put them in the bath water; after a tiring day, immerse yourself in the warm water of a bathtub to which an amber has been added, stimulates our vitality.

Aquamarine

Aquamarine is a stone useful for physical and mental balance, also effective for self-esteem and fulfillment.
The name of the aquamarine stone comes from the Latin word "aqua marina" which means "water of the sea", and ancient sailors believed that the stone could help protect them from drowning and ensure a good catch of fish.
An excellent stone for fluid retention, aquamarine is associated with the thyme gland and recommended as a throat purifier and sore throat.
Aquamarine is a very important stone for decreasing anxiety, fear, restlessness and obtaining a peaceful mind.
- From a purely metaphysical point of view, this fascinating stone activates the Throat Chakra, 5th chakra, thus facilitating perfect communication of one's real interiority; not only that: it has the great faculty of helping communication, both on a physical and ethereal level, with the other beings of creation, especially with those who inhabit the waters of the sea.

Also called the "Stone of Courage", the energy it emanates not only appeases emotions such as anger, but accentuates one's intellectual faculties and has the ability to increase the forces of the mind.
To obtain long-lasting effects on the spiritual level, it is advisable to always carry the aquamarine in close contact with the skin, especially near the throat.
As far as physical therapy is concerned, a crystal can be placed directly on the eyelids in case of pain or strain in the eyes.
At night, however, you can place the aquamarine under your pillow to sleep peacefully.
Aquamarine can be combined in the following ways:
- With stellerite, blue cavansite, green diopside and lepidocrocite to help manage negative emotions.
- With aura water to improve communication.

- With blue aragonite, amazonite, sodalite, chrysocolla, blue calcite and larimar to enhance communication with the Divine.
- With labradorite, iolite, blue aventurine, blue apatite and lepidocrocite to enhance your intuitive and psychic abilities.
- With morganite to strengthen love and compassion.

Aquamarine is mainly found in Brazil, Russia (Ural Mountains) and Madagascar, but there are also several deposits in Nigeria, USA (California), South Africa, China, Australia, the Middle East and South East Asia.

Agate

Agate is the most creative crystal with stripes that nature could create. It is a stone linked to relaxation, tranquility, inner cleansing, balance, meditation, vitality, concreteness, pain relief and balancing between Yin and Yang energies. Very useful for keeping nightmares and fears away.
- In crystal healing agate finds the perfect use in treating those people who need to maintain a good balance through sensible choices, whatever the area of life (love, work, family, health, friends) that is causing a energy imbalance.

It seems that the agate not only protects against forms of negative energy, but performs the function of a casing that stabilizes and harmonizes every single organ and cell of the body. It has a particular protective action towards pregnant women. It is also indicated in case of conjunctivitis and problems with the gastrointestinal tract.
- On a mental level this volcanic stone offers a sense of security and protection that you will hardly find in other stones. The role that has been attributed to it for centuries is precisely this, accompanied by the ability to make the person who uses it more confident in their own possibilities.

Agate can be worn as a pendant during the day and hung by the bed at night.
- The streaked gray, streaked black and natural qualities act on the 1st chakra.
- The striped quality with a prevalence of orange works on the 2nd chakra.
- The predominantly yellow quality works on the 3rd chakra.
- The streaked green and pink qualities act on the 4th chakra.

Fuchsia agate

The properties of the Fuchsia Agate allow you to let go of the disappointments and the deep sadness that creeps into us; you just have to look at it and play with it.
In particular, it helps to manifest one's perspicacity and allows to stimulate analytical capacity, thus providing a good balance between one's physical, emotional and spiritual bodies.

Moss agate

Moss Agate, despite its name, contains very little organic material, moss or lichens, but the particular green shapes are mainly due to various mineral inclusions.
Traditionally Moss Agate can aid the body in long term illnesses, and is also known to aid circulation and the lymphatic system.
It has the ability to strengthen the immune system, eliminating harmful waste from the tissues and respiratory tract. Acting as a good anti-inflammatory, its use is excellent for the treatment of colds, fever, cough and various inflammations including those of the skeletal and joint system as well as for the treatment of diabetes.
The Chakra associated with it is the 4th, that of the Heart.

Fire Agate

Red stones are related to lower chakras and help give courage. They improve grounding and calm fears. On a physical level it is linked to the circulatory, nervous and endocrine systems. Free from energy blocks.

Blue Agate

Like all blue stones it is connected from the point of view of chromotherapy to the 5th chakra, that of the throat; therefore, it is the perfect agate for you if you wish to improve your communication skills, removing those emotional traumas that could interfere with the success of a performance. It is a strongly feminine stone and is often given to pregnant women to protect them and wish them a peaceful pregnancy.

Botswana agate

Also known as eye agate, Botswana agate is able to retain sunlight, so that it can then be given to those who are lost. The color of Botswana Agate ranges from gray to pink. It forms a striated structure which enhances its protective effect. Pink color soothes feelings, stimulating the emergence of new relationships. Gray on the other hand is the color of magic, of inner silence that leads to awareness. Stimulates sensuality and helps overcome anxieties. Thanks to the silver-colored inclusions, it stimulates reflection.

- Botswana Agate is the ideal stone for those who want to quit smoking. Just use it as an elixir, i.e. immerse it for a few hours in water and then drink it.

Alexandrite

Alexandrite, one of the rarest stones that exist on our planet, has the main characteristic of being iridescent, that is, it has the ability to change color when illuminated.
- Considered the stone of the Scorpio astrological sign, it has the gift of keeping our emotional level under control. Furthermore, in difficult situations, it strengthens the intuition of the wearer: in fact, it seems to give the power to find solutions that logic, at first glance, does not seem to give.

Its ability to change color, from green-brown or bluish green when exposed to natural light, to red-violet and red-grey, makes this stone unique in its kind, and for this reason, also very expensive.

Aluminum, iron and chromium are the main elements of the stone:
- Aluminum is indicated for mental development delays, memory impairment and insomnia.
- Iron is needed to oxygenate tissue cells.
- Chromium stimulates the synthesis of fatty acids and helps reduce the arteriosclerotic process.

The Chakra with which it is connected is the 2nd, that of the Pelvic Center while the zodiac sign to which it is linked is Scorpio.

Amazonite

Amazonite properties are used for artistic creativity and energy healing.
It is an excellent stone for communication, trust and leadership; reduces self-harming behaviors, increases self-respect, grace, self-confidence with external communication.
- The benefits of amazonite are calming for the brain and nervous system, helping to filter information and combine it with natural intuition to enhance understanding, and to improve one's ability to cooperate with others, as well as the ability to express themselves.

Excellent stone to improve skin condition, and smooth wrinkles; through contact with amazonite, arthritis, rheumatism and cervical pain will benefit.
- It is suggested to use Amazonite in combination with Atlantisite, Jade and Chalcopyrite.

Considered a lucky stone, especially by players, Amazonite has the great ability to calm the mood swings of the soul, thus acting as a tranquilizer; it also enormously increases decision-making power, making the person who wears it safer and free from fears from the outside world. The consequence of this is the great facility to create and lead intense interpersonal relationships.
- Amazonite, in practice, gives a strong balance to Yin and Yang energies. Its therapeutic faculties are many: suitable for relieving sore throats and respiratory tract diseases in general, it is well suited to pregnant women and to those who, due to daily stress, experience the first symptoms of a nervous breakdown.

But its properties do not end there:
- Has relaxing properties for the muscles, especially after making great efforts.

- Helps the liver to metabolize foods that are difficult to absorb.
- Helps the relaxation of the whole body, relieving the sense of tiredness.
- At an endocrine and hormonal level, it harmonizes the functions of the pituitary and thymus while at a neuronal level, it regulates the vegetative system.

Amber

The word Amber comes from the Arabic Anbar which, initially, indicated a waxy substance produced by the stomach of the Sperm Whale. Obviously, the Amber that we know does not refer to that type of product, but to a mixture of fossilized organic compounds (resins). The first resin produced by trees, ancestors of the current conifers, dates back to around 250 million years ago, i.e. in the Mesozoic period.
The resin, produced by very large trees, was deposited on the ground starting the first phase of fossilization called polymerization. The next process, called precisely fossilization, takes place after about 5 million years, resulting in that substance, with a glassy appearance, called Amber.
Amber, to be defined as such, must be at least 150,000 years old, otherwise it is Copal or Copalite which are organic resins that are not old enough (less than 100,000 years) and not yet fossilized and hardened enough to become amber.

- Amber has always been considered a highly protective and anti-demon amulet. Highly protective, it also helps in the manifestation of one's ideas in everyday reality. It strengthens the solar plexus, gives mental clarity, balance and confidence in one's own possibilities. Amber can help metabolism deficiencies, hearing problems and stomach ailments.
- In Poland tincture of amber is still considered an effective remedy for colds, throat and respiratory problems. Amber powder is inhaled to bring relief to respiratory problems.

The life force within amber promotes fertility and its protective and environmental clearing properties make it a remedy to be used to prepare for a healing or motherhood. Amber gives bright energy that is calming and energizing at the same time. Regenerates the environment by drawing out heavy negativity when burned.

Amber is excellent when accompanied by jaietto, fossil jasper and carnelian.
- Amber has the power to transmute negative energies into positive energies.

But, beyond this great faculty, it is used as a sedative of the entire nervous system. Amber also amplifies one's predispositions and intellectual abilities.
- In general it is thought that this "stone" can act on our entire body by purifying our energies by infusing us with a deep sense of warmth.
- This means that our body is always protected from possible ailments.

The chakra associated with it is the 3rd, that of the navel and the solar plexus, while its zodiac sign is Leo.
Remember to always clean and purify amber if used for crystal healing practices and never leave amber in the sun as it can become brittle.

Amethyst

Amethyst is widely used to open the spiritual and psychic energy centers and this makes it one of the most important power stones. Amethyst symbolizes compassion, humility, sincerity and spiritual wisdom.
The amethyst gives common sense and flexibility in decisions, strengthens and improves psychic, intuitive and clairvoyant abilities being energetically directly connected with the energy of our mind.
- Excellent detoxifying stone, amethyst helps with addictions and calms the nervous system by promoting the transmission of signals within it.
- Amethyst is an energy transmuter, it helps to open doors into intense and transformative spiritual experiences.
- Excellent stone for the Third Eye chakra and the Crown chakra.

One of its peculiarities is to purify other stones; in fact, it is recommended to use it in combination with other stones or crystals.
- Helps perceive the spiritual aspect behind the events. Thus, the Amethyst manages to be a good remedy for reworking a mourning and the consequent pain due to the loss of the loved one. It also increases the sense of justice, humility and honesty.

It is an effective calmer for the mind, which promotes concentration and calms confused thoughts. Amethyst has the ability to relieve feelings of guilt, strengthening self-confidence and decreasing inferiority complexes. Its influence on the emotional sphere is expressed by helping to calm the emotionality, favoring greater clarity.
It is an effective remedy against insomnia and nightmares so as to promote deep rest; the result is the reduction of tensions with the consequent reduction of migraines.

The dark variety mitigates hypertension and stiffness and is an excellent regulator of bacterial flora.
- Works in great synergy with Bach Flowers, in particular with the Agrimony remedy.

Amethyst is an excellent remedy for rebalancing the energy of environments, especially bedrooms and rooms where we welcome people who do not belong to our family.
- They are also used in medical offices such as, for example, psychologists, where many people come to vent by talking about their problems and therefore the environment is affected by negative energies that must be driven away.

The zodiac signs associated with this stone are Sagittarius, Capricorn and Pisces, while the corresponding Chakra is the 6th, or the Third Eye, and the 7th, the Crown Chakra.

Ametrine

The stone name Ametrine comes from the powerful combination of Amethyst and Citrine, connecting realms between the physical and the spiritual; Ametrine is a rare and unusual stone that occurs when citrine also resides in amethyst quartz.
- Its dual nature makes it very effective in removing energy blockages in each chakra, helping to achieve a healthy psychophysical balance.

Ametrine has an effect on the general well-being and mental health of people suffering from depression, mood swings and anxiety, has a calming effect on mood and increases feelings of tranquility. An excellent meditation stone, Ametrine tunes into higher states of consciousness naturally inducing meditation and helping to more quickly achieve calmness and new perceptions to discover our greatest potential.
- Ametrine strengthens the oxygen in our body.

An ametrine elixir can help remove toxins from the body and be helpful in reducing or alleviating some of the symptoms of physical illnesses.
Ametrine reconciles our spiritual aspirations very well with worldly life; it is often used during meditation and reiki and crystal therapy treatments.
The Chakras corresponding to this stone are the 6th, the Third Eye and the 7th, the Crown Chakra.

Angelite

This stone allows for excellent balancing and polarization for the alignment of the physical body with the Aura.
It's an excellent stone to use when you need to calm down from feelings of anger and overwhelm; thus, it gives a great inner calm, relieves emotional stress, gives peace and eliminates negative and distorted visions that often manifest themselves in our lives causing unconscious fears, fixed ideas or unclear thoughts.
- Its properties on the body, therefore, mirror those of the mind, relieving all physical reactions from states of anger or strong emotions such as inflammation, digestive and intestinal allergies or the same emotional problems.

Angelite is soluble in water and therefore absolutely must not be cleaned in water.
Angelite supports the functionality of the kidneys; it is used for bone growth and in the treatment of diseases associated with them such as arthritis and osteoporosis, as well as to promote self-healing towards problems due to trauma.
The Chakras combined with Angelite are the 2nd, 5th and 6th:
- For the 5th Chakra located in the center of the throat, it helps the latter eliminate inflammation and energy excesses, giving positive energy in communication with others.

An energizing but more revitalizing effect is given by the combination with the 6th Chakra, that of the Third Eye while as regards the one with the 2nd Chakra, of the Pelvic Center, it has an unblocking action on the same.

Antimonite

Antimonite, through its energetic vibrations, helps to reconcile one's personal interests in the social and material fields with spiritual interests and expressions, thus helping both artistic-creative and aesthetic abilities.
On the physical level, Antimonite helps the healing of gastrointestinal disorders such as nausea, vomiting and gastritis; it is widely used for the treatment of epidermis pathologies such as itching, dry skin, wrinkles, dandruff or psoriasis (the cure is recommended by associating it with sulfur water).

- Antimonite should always be carried with you, preferably in a natural fiber bag, since its fragility does not allow it to be mounted on a pendant or any other support. To best benefit from the properties of Antimonite, it is useful to introduce it into the cover of the pillow in which you sleep so that the beneficial vibrations act more intensely during sleep.

The chakra most responsive to its vibrations is the 1st, located in the center of the root.

Apatite

It is a stone considered a powerful source of emotional inspiration; it is able to develop psychic abilities and gently attunes us to our spiritual level.
Apatite can enhance one's intuition, learning ability and mental creativity, and can instill greater self-confidence.
- May assist in attaining deeper states of meditation and, when used with other stones and crystals, may more rapidly facilitate desired results as well as enhance their purpose.
- It is useful for bones, calcium absorption, cartilage, teeth and motor skills in general.

It can also be used for energetic cleaning of the environments where we live or stay more often; placing apatite in front of the windows and near the entrance door can help to better convey the flow of positive energies, greatly improving the surrounding environment.
- Excellent stone to better regulate sleep and rest times, apatite is also a stone of benefit for all those who are close and in contact with nature, managing to infuse the healing energies of nature itself, wherever you go.

The action of Apatite on the body is of a tonic type: in fact, it favors the appetite and gives tone to the tissues, regenerating the cells especially of the skeletal system, helping in case of fractures, arthrosis, rickets and osteoporosis.
The chakras associated with it are the 3rd for the yellow variety, the 4th chakra for the green one and the 5th chakra for the blue one.

Apophyllite

Apophyllite helps to get rid of all emotional tensions coming from the subconscious due to stress, bad relationship with oneself and with others, favoring altruism and generosity. It helps to face life's problems with more calm and serenity, curbing fears and depressive thoughts in which there seems to be no solution.

- Helps to see situations in a better light, increasing self-esteem and a more prejudice-free view of one's way of being and perceiving emotions more clearly.
- On the physical level it is useful to help cure problems of the respiratory system.
- This stone is also used for the treatment of asthma and allergies as well as for nervous system dysfunctions.

It is also used in synergy with Cherry Plum, a Bach flower remedy, or during reiki treatments, meditation or crystal therapy sessions.

The Chakras in harmony with this stone are in the case of the green-water color the 5th Chakra and in the case of the white one, the 7th Chakra, i.e. that of the Crown.

Aragonite

The properties of aragonite direct energy towards self-discipline, helping to persevere despite the limitations that life often has before us; it helps us better understand that these limitations represent the way we interact with the world and life, and often determine our spiritual and physical growth.
Aragonite has historically been used to banish the heat of fevers, reduce inflammation and calm the nervous system.
- It has the ability to increase energy vibrationally, in particular, it can increase the energy of prayers and magical amulets.

Aragonite is known to work synergistically with pyrite, calcite, and all types of jasper.
Depending on its coloring, it manages to have beneficial influences on different spheres of life.
- The white and blue color is an excellent calming of too impetuous mental processes that are reflected on the nervous system such as stress, anxiety, invasive recurring thoughts, fatigue.
- Orange is a good remedy for small or large emotional traumas, helping to unblock the energy nodes related to the thought processing cycle and consequently favors concentration.

Aragonite, therefore, helps to open a glimmer of altruism, generosity and understanding in relationships with others.
The chakra with which it has an energetic correspondence is the 7th, that of the Crown for the white type, the 2nd chakra for the orange one and the 5th chakra for the light blue variety.

Astrophyllite

Astrophyllite is a great energy condenser both physically and metaphysically; in fact, it is capable of instilling energy into the meridian chakras, the aura and the superior bodies, increasing our dream activity.
Astrophyllite is a catalyst of psychic energies: it helps openness towards others, favoring verbal and empathic communication.
In the physical sphere it acts as a stimulant of the hormonal system, thus helping to overcome midlife crises, problems related to the menstrual cycle and the large intestine.

- One of the best ways to experience the energizing power of this stone is to introduce it into the pillowcase you sleep on; this amplifies the potential of the dream activity.

The 6th chakra is the one with the greatest compatibility with Astrophyllite, the Third Eye but it is also excellent to place it behind the knees.

Atlantisite

Atlantisite is the combination of green serpentine with pink to purple inclusions of stichtite from Tasmania and, as such, blends the characteristics of both these crystals together. In Atlantisite there is a unique combination of colors including yellow-green-purple-purple that occur only at the "Stichtite Hill" quarry at the top of a small hill in Zeehan, Tasmania, where it is mined exclusive. The name Atlantisite comes from Atlantis, the lost city that Plato was the first to write about.
- Atlantisite is an ideal crystal to work on the third eye chakra and heart chakra, to heighten our perceptions and feeling of unconditional love.

It helps us to naturally establish our energetic and psychic "boundaries". It can help unruly children and adults change their behavior patterns.
- It comforts those who live alone and helps us to be kind to ourselves and to others.
- It is also an excellent stone for protection from negative energies and is useful in appropriate meditation, to raise one's Kundalini.

Atlantisite's properties allow psychic access to retrieve ancient wisdom and information, or images, about past lives allowing the spiritual journey of the person using it to proceed at the person's pace.

Atlantisite can promote skin elasticity and regeneration and is useful in the treatment of hernias.

Aventurine

Green aventurine is comparable to the lucky four-leaf clover: it is often placed in bags to keep close to bring abundance and good luck in money.
Aventurine is also used in spells and ritual magic.
- Aventurine stone has the ability to enhance its user's sense of humor and gaiety. It's also an excellent balancing stone, it gives inner balance and stimulates dreams.
- Has a positive effect on the psyche, reinforcing a sense of individualism, and is the ideal stone for those seeking a positive outlook on life.

It can help balance the innermost and dormant emotions (great combination with malachite) and is one of the best stones to wear or carry during times of stress.
It is also historically known for being able to bring out the heat of fever and inflammation.
- If we use more aventurine stones in the bath water, they become stones for calming emotional pain and fears, managing to dissolve blockages in the heart chakra.

On the spiritual side, Aventurine is an excellent aid in understanding where our life is moving and what choices we must make to pursue our true path.
- The corresponding chakra is the 4th, that of the Heart.
- The zodiac signs associated with it are Taurus, Cancer, Sagittarius and Scorpio.

Its different colors are associated with different qualities: Red Aventurine gives a more cheerful vision of life, raises the vital state and promotes good interpersonal relationships and sexual life; in fact, the Aventurine of this coloring is very useful for the treatment of disorders of the reproductive system.

The sign of Scorpio is especially associated with this Aventurine.

As for Green Aventurine, its properties are more calming and aimed at the nervous system; it acts excellently on tachycardia and stress and is a good remedy for skin pathologies due to nervous problems.

The zodiac signs associated with this variety are Taurus, Cancer and Sagittarius.

Azurite

The azurite stone is a crystal that manages to expand the limits of the conscious sphere, promoting a healthy re-evaluation of one's abilities and hidden talents. It also can help unite the subconscious with the conscious mind by expanding the limits of our mind. Azurite is an ideal stone to hold when starting to meditate.
- Azurite has the property of alleviating recurring worries, phobias and annoying negative thoughts, bringing our attention to recognize the areas of greatest need.
- Instills intellectual logic with love, promoting compassion for self and others.
- May help stimulate the thyroid gland, cleanse the skin, spleen and etheric bodies.
- Excellent stone to help control and direct the flow of energy and bring the right amount of it to any situation.

The properties of azurite make it a beautiful stone for the third eye chakra, awakening psychic abilities and helping to recognize appropriate spiritual guidance when it presents itself.
Used with the throat chakra, the fifth chakra, it can promote communication with the heart and increase awareness of the spiritual path undertaken.
Always carry with you in a natural fiber bag.
The chakra associated with it is the 6th, that of the Third Eye, and the 5th chakra, that of the Throat.

Biotite

Biotite is a very dark stone found in nature in laminates or aggregates. Its energetic properties give strength and vitality, promoting self-realization, adaptability and creativity which justify why it is considered the stone of women in childbirth.
- Biotite, in fact, favors childbirth, decreasing the pain of labor as it relaxes the mouth of the uterus.

On a strictly psychological level, Biotite frees from taboos and negative mental patterns, sometimes self-destructive, which cause suffering, thus helping to have a clearer and more intuitive mind to resolve situations or make decisions more clearly.

Another quality of Biotite is the protection against thoughts full of negative energy coming from others and all those environmental influences that tend to distance us from our true personality.

Its function on the body is purifying and decongestant, helping to cure sciatica, purifying the blood from uric acids, thus freeing from gout and facilitating the functioning of the kidneys.
- It is energetically compatible with the 1st chakra in the black variety, with the 7th chakra in the silver variety and with the 4th chakra in the presence of the green variety.

The associated zodiac sign is Scorpio.

Blenda

Blenda, or Sphalerite, is a stone that renews stagnant psychic energies; its use, in fact, allows the removal of old ideas, fears or traumas deriving from past experiences. It favors both mental and psychic regeneration, giving the necessary strength to recover during the dark periods of our lives.

- With the use of this stone, thoughts become more lucid and projected towards good and spirituality while our interpersonal relationships become more spontaneous and stimulating.

Blenda promotes good sleep and greater concentration and intuition in order to achieve one's goals and dreams. Blenda is an excellent balancer of the endocrine system; strengthens the immune system and the retina of the eye. Widely used for diabetes and skin care; it also has a good action on the central nervous system, reactivating the senses such as smell and taste.

The Blenda is increasingly used in synergy with a flower of the Bach remedies, the Honeysuckle, 3-4 days after taking the remedy.

The Chakra associated with it is the 3rd one of the navel center. A good habit is to fix it with a plaster in correspondence with the energy center of the chakra.

Boji Stone

The Boji Stone helps balance the energy fields of the human body by performing a function similar to that of acupuncture, so much so that it is optimally compatible with all chakras or energy centers. The main property of the Boji Stone is the reconciliation of opposites: masculine-feminine, spirit-matter, in such a way as to best express the most genuine part of ourselves through the emergence of unconscious dreams and desires. Precisely for this reason that, during use, two should always be used; one energetically masculine and the other energetically feminine. The male stone differs from the female one due to its rougher appearance with crystallizations and protuberances (although very rarely you can find "hermaphrodite" stones with a part of the smooth shell and one with a rough shell).
- Precisely because of this duality, the Boji Stone is excellent for balancing our way of seeing life, giving a more material vision to those who need to see life in a more realistic way and having a more carefree and imaginative vision for those who he sees the more materialistic and serious side. The consequence is the expression of our unmanifested characteristics and creative abilities.

The Boji Stone should be used holding it in both hands: the female stone should be held in the male energy part of the human body, i.e. on the right, while the male one should be held in the left hand relating to the female energy part.
The Boji Stone is associated with the zodiac signs of Aquarius, Scorpio, Taurus and Leo.

Chalcedony

Chalcedony is closely linked to ritual magic, so much so that in the 16th century it was prescribed, worn around the neck or with them by magicians to dissolve illusions and fantasies.
More Chalcedony stones were commonly used to ward off black magic, psychic attacks, and other negative ritual magic created especially for people.
Chalcedony is a stone that symbolizes calmness and composure.
For the Tibetans it is a stone of purity, strong concentration and internalization of the essential.
Chalcedony gives nourishment to the soul, promotes brotherhood and goodwill, and enhances group stability.
Can be used to facilitate telepathy. Chalcedony can give feelings of benevolence and generosity, eliminating regressed hostilities allowing melancholy to transform into joy.
- Chalcedony properties increase vitality, stamina and promote emotional balance and charity. It can relieve fever, gallstones and eye problems.

In particular, chalcedony is used in Russia by mothers to increase milk during breastfeeding.
Chalcedony is used by healers alongside other stones to amplify their effects, especially if one is working towards spiritual wholeness and personal development..

Yellow calcite

Calcite owes its name to the Latin word "calx" which means "lime", given that for calcite the main component is limestone. There is a deep connection between yellow calcite stone and that of the animal and plant kingdoms and throughout nature, the real ability to move forward despite external influences by taking an active part in what we are creating in our lives.
- Yellow Calcite stone is well known for its propensity for purification, cleansing and in tune with the regenerating and revitalizing power of nature itself.
- Yellow Calcite is used to remove old patterns (blockages) of old stagnant energy in us and to increase personal motivation and sense of unity.
- Yellow calcite is an excellent stone for studying the arts and sciences and for amplifying and increasing any type of energy, thanks to the double refractive property discovered in the stone in 1669 by Erasmo Bartholinus.

Yellow Calcite can help bones and joints and balance the amount of calcium in the body, helping to improve the absorption of important vitamins and minerals in the body.
The properties of yellow calcite are a good aid for remote energy work, given the amplifying power that can be sent.

Celestine

Celestine, from the Latin "caelestis" which means "celestial", was so named for its very ethereal appearance.
Celestina is a stone of peace and harmony which induces a vision of real peaceful coexistence with the entire universe.
Also called "heaven stone", due to its soft celestial color, it was believed to have been created by choirs of Heavenly Angels.

- In New Age circles celestine is said to be native to the stars known as the Pleiades (commonly referred to as the "Seven Sisters") and that the stone holds celestial wisdom.
- Celestine has a very high frequency and is a very spiritual stone that can help open portals to one's Higher Self.

Known for expanding creativity it is often used in the arts. Accelerates spiritual development and brings a general sense of peace.

Kyanite

It is a stone that is highly recommended to be in the collection of those who do spiritual work on themselves.

- Kyanite does not accumulate negative energies and vibrations, therefore, it almost never needs to be cleaned and purified. Since kyanite's energy is limitless, it is said to be one of the best crystals to use as an attunement stone.

- Kyanite is a powerful amplifier of high frequency energy, suitable for meditation and soul ascension. It is a stone for connection to the higher realms and helps one to understand the true purpose of life.

Kyanite has a strong calming effect on the whole being bringing inner tranquility and peace; encourages the formation of psychic skills and communication on all levels, therefore, great for the throat and fifth chakra.

Kyanite drives away anger, frustration and mental confusion and helps to give a logical and linear thinking ability. Kyanite provides a clear stimulating energy, aiding perseverance and support in the work of one's Self, and in everyday activities and situations that normally deplete one's strength.

In addition, kyanite helps when connecting with one's spirit guides, and induces lucid dreaming by promoting dreams of healing. It is used to treat hearing disorders, eye disorders, as well as problems with the sense of smell. These characteristics make kyanite an excellent choice for any type of energy work.

Coral

Coral, as we know, is not part of the mineral world; coral, in fact, is made up of communities of small polyps which form, at the base of their soft body, a calcium carbonate skeleton with a protective and supportive function.
Since time immemorial, man has been looking for this marine gem as a symbol of beauty and a source of regenerating energy.
Red Coral, also called "Blood Stone" gives a sense of aggregation, eluding tensions and reticence created by past experiences.

- Character or psychological problems disappear with Coral's help, so that our life opens up to more collaborative and fulfilling experiences, where communication is not difficult and anxieties, suspicions and shyness appear further away and less limiting.
- Coral hardens the entire skeletal system and the body in general.
- Red Coral, in particular, is used in the treatment of osteoporosis. The madrepora coral is legally available on the market.

Fossil Coral has the same abilities as non-fossilized coral even if it has changed its organic parts to quartzite.
The chakra compatible with it is the 2nd, the sacral center and the zodiac sign associated with it is Scorpio.

Carnelian

Carnelian helps in understanding the inner self, strengthens and motivates concentration, helps in public speaking, increasing one's self-esteem.
- It is a stone of power and can bring success in one's life.

Carnelian is used to counteract negative thoughts and doubts, and wearing this stone can prevent others from reading thoughts or influencing one's mind.
- Carnelian is also mentioned in the Egyptian Book of the Dead, to be placed in tombs as "magic armor" for life after death.

The ancient Egyptians associated it with the goddess Isis because of her red color; the goddess, finding the limbs of her beloved husband Osiris, killed by her brother Set, reassembled them, bringing him back to life.
From this legend Carnelian is thought to have the same vital and energetic properties as blood, instilling courage to face fears, including that of death.
Another famous amulet that uses carnelian is the Eye of Horus, which is believed to offer protection against the evil eye.
Carnelian is often used for blood purification, facilitating its flow into tissues and organs so as to help the assimilation of vitamins.
- Among other properties, it helps the elimination of toxins from the body, the stimulation of the small intestine and metabolism as well as the treatment of diarrhea and all intestinal problems in general, favoring digestion.
- Carnelian is used to relieve kidney pain, for the treatment of asthma and for problems with the abdomen and bladder; it is even used for the treatment of cystitis and prostate problems and the entire urinary tract.

Among other qualities we can include the ability to cure infertility, to facilitate the resolution of problems with the uterus, to strengthen the eyes, the gums and to make the skin younger and more elastic. During pregnancy it is advisable to place it on the belly because this brings serenity to the unborn child.

Corniola has a very slow but decisive action; for this reason it must be used in a very long time.

The Chakra associated with it is the 2nd.

Crysocolla

Some ancient American Indian tribes used chrysocolla for its ability to strengthen the body's resistance to the elements and to bring that feeling of inner calm to those upset by emotional and emotional turmoil. In ancient Egypt, chrysocolla was called the "Sage's Stone" as it was often used by members of the royal council, traders and those negotiating. For this Queen Cleopatra carried chrysocolla jewelry with her wherever she went.

- Chrysocolla is a soothing and calming stone for times of greatest stress, even just the sight of it brings about inner balance and a gentle soul, calming emotions and bringing understanding between discordant relationships.
- Chrysocolla is a powerful source of vital energy, with a pronounced feminine energy, and helps to free the subconscious from deep-seated negative feelings of guilt and to transform historical resentment in people.

Chrysocolla stone can relieve cramps, throat infections and used on the sixth chakra offers immense spiritual benefits.
The properties of chrysocolla allow you to enhance creativity and revitalize all chakras by aligning them with the Divine.

- In case of fever, it stimulates the lowering of the temperature; heals from burns or infections.

It can also be used simultaneously with a Bach Scleranthus remedy.
The compatible chakra is the 5th, the Throat Center and the associated zodiac sign is Libra.

Jasper

Jasper is a microcrystalline variety of quartz; it is generally red in color but jaspers are very frequent with streaks or patches of another color due to the presence of foreign substances.
- A particular variety of jasper is the dark green heliotrope with reddish patches due to the presence of iron hydroxide. It is thought that jasper can be a circulatory rebalancer by acting on the iron in hemoglobin.

Jasper strengthens the liver, gallbladder, bladder and kidneys. It is a powerful therapeutic, protects against disease and has the greatest impact on the physical body, which is strengthened. It regulates the healing of the gastric system and brings balance to the endocrine system.
- Resistant, solid, reassuring, jasper is the stone of stability, as it represents the Earth element.

On a subtle level it should be considered as the connecting stone between the "sacred and profane" of every human being, in practice between pure instinct and intuition. Jasper strengthens faith in ideals and helps to make the necessary efforts to transform intentions into deeds.
Works with the chakras depending on the color of the stone:
- The red variety and the brecciated one act on the 2nd chakra.
- The yellow variety works on the 3rd chakra.
- The green variety stimulates the 4th chakra.

Red Jasper

Jasper, in all its variants, is a unique stone that removes all negative energy present in the human body.
Red Jasper is the most powerful variety: it stimulates the circulation of energy in the body.

Works on blood when there is a problem of infection or congenital anemia. Stimulates the reproductive organs, rebalances the sexual energies. Fortifies the fetus. Facilitates childbirth making it less painful and problematic.
- Supports the wearer and supports them during times of greatest stress, bringing a sense of tranquility and wholeness.
- It is also a stone of deep personal fairness and justice, strengthening accountability, better choices for our evolution, and compassion.
- It can have a stabilizing effect, and can help you regain all your energy and help you use it in a more balanced way. Red Jasper aids in all critical survival areas, and of course, is an excellent stone of protection.

It relieves the pains of the gastrointestinal tract, and reduces the pain of hematomas. Great for women's issues. Helps with blood, anemia, hemorrhages, and juvenile rashes. It can foster a deep connection with life and with the earth. Carrying it with you inspires a positive and joyful attitude by increasing creative action. Works well in combination with black and green stones.

Heliotrope

Heliotrope has been used since ancient times to increase personal energy and physical strength. Instills calm, especially in survival situations, and increases adaptability and organizational power, decreasing confusion and anxiety.

- Often used to cleanse and detoxify the body, it cleanses the lower chakras, realigning their energies.

Heliotrope has always been used in ritual magic.

In ancient Babylon, it was used in rituals against enemies and in ancient Egypt used to open space-time gates and break ties.

Heliotrope can help enhance intuition and creativity, and can be used to combat fatigue and confusion.

It is good to keep a heliotrope in any place where its energy needs to be very clean. Even today heliotrope is used as a medicine and aphrodisiac in India.

Hematite

Hematite in ancient Egypt was used to buffer blood and promote blood cell formation.
In the Middle Ages hematite was called "bloodstone" due to the fact that water turned red in contact with the mineral and it was customary to wear hematite jewelery during a mourning.
- It's an excellent rooting stone, it strengthens the body and improves resistance to emotional stress; it is a powerful stone that helps to endure the trials and vicissitudes of life.
- Hematite, besides its association with blood, is also known to be a stone for the mind.
- Creates mental organization and concentration and will help us in logical thinking and mathematics. It can stimulate iron absorption and improve oxygen supply to the body, normalizing blood pressure and body weight.

The properties of hematite to reflect all negativity where it came from are known to magicians and exorcists; gives reliable protection against the evil eye and black magic.
Used together with black tourmaline and shungite, hematite protects against geopathic stress and electromagnetic smog, as well as negativity, psychic attacks and ritual magic, returning what was sent back to the sender.
Curiosity: in the past the hematite was used for the construction of the magic mirror.

Fluorite

Excellent stone for strengthening bones, teeth and improving pain associated with arthritis. Fluorite helps revive sexual appetite. The properties of Fluorite make it possible to protect wellness operators or anyone who is in close contact with many people from psychic manipulation, voluntary or otherwise. In different parts of the world Fluorite was thought to be the "home of the rainbow" due to the mixed colors present in it.

- Fluorite can help increase concentration and intuition. It can implement to remain impartial when the decisions must not involve us emotionally.
- Fluorite stone is highly protective and functions as an energy stabilizer.
- Absorbs negative energies from the environment and is effective for our Aura and Chakra cleaning.
- Helps grasp higher concepts, is a formidable stone for college students and researchers who need to analyze data and come to conclusions.

In particular, it allows for innovation and inventiveness, being a very effective stone to use for mental creativity and for creating wealth and prosperity.
Fluorite works excellently with all stones, especially agate and carnelian.

Galena

One of the oldest uses of the galena stone was for cosmetic purposes; in ancient Egypt, in fact, it was used to apply it around the eyes to reduce the glare of the desert sun and to repel flies, which were a potential source of disease.
The galena stone offers good grounding and improves the perception of subtle energies in ourselves and in others. Galena is a stone of strong personal harmony, stimulates interaction on all levels, and helps reduce limiting thoughts, but at the same time teaches us to accept our limits. Promotes holistic maturity, relationship with nature and animals. It is used to open doors between the physical body and other subtle bodies, to allow for the alignment and circulation of energies, while also stimulating the nervous system.

- Galena is a strong stone of transformation and its effective energy is manifested when one embarks on a personal spiritual journey, fostering receptivity and giving the courage and ability to tackle initially difficult tasks.
- Galena can help counteract radiation and electromagnetic pollution and other forms of heavy environmental energy.
- May help reduce inflammation and rashes, circulation problems and hair growth.

Galena allows you to maintain a constant connection with the Divine, even in the darkest places and moments.
Galena, combined with Labradorite, is used for deep inner healing, while it is excellent when combined with black Tourmaline and Shungite, for personal protection from any "unwelcome" energy.

Jade

Jade is among the oldest objects found from antiquity dating back to about 7,000 years ago and given its hardness, it was used to produce weapons and ritual knives.

The working of jade in China (called "yu") has continued uninterruptedly for 5,000 years to create finely crafted objects of worship, since jade, in Chinese tradition, symbolizes the five virtues of humanity:
- The wisdom.
- Compassion.
- Justice.
- Modesty.
- The bravery.

Jade is especially helpful for those who react to changes in weather conditions, it greatly stabilizes and balances the masculine and feminine energy of the wearer.
- Jade is a stone that can help achieve our goals by instilling resourcefulness and allows us to see beyond our self-imposed limitations and manifest our ideas in the physical world.
- The jade stone is considered a stone that helps and propitiates economic luck.

The properties of jade (preferably together with amber and chalcopyrite) are very protective and particularly suitable for children against childhood diseases.
It is excellent if you want to experience more vivid dreams, while if you want to gain a greater understanding of psychic dreams, try sleeping with jade under your pillow or on your nightstand for a while.

Garnet

Garnet is found in the form of jewelry in various ancient cultures such as the ancient Egyptians, Greeks and Romans.
Garnet in Vedic astrology has long been a talisman used to ward off evil influences from the celestial body called Rahu. Historically, it was believed to give protection from wounds and poison and to stop bleeding from wounds.

- Particularly the Eastern belief that the garnet holds not only the power to protect its user from negative energies manifested by others, but to repel these negative energies to those who originated them. Garnet can be beneficial for total body and soul shielding.

As a stone of moderation it can be used to balance the sacral chakra and excessive sexual desire and to promote the controlled growth of the Kundalini, inspiring love and passion, devotion and loyalty but also constancy in friendships. When garnet is used in conjunction with ametrine or kyanite, it can help provide past life information.
Peculiarity of the garnet is the calming of internal, and non-manifest, anger that one possesses towards oneself.

Howlite

Howlite stone is named after Henry How, a Canadian chemist, geologist and mineralist who classified it in 1868 and discovered it in Nova Scotia. Howlite stone is known for its strong associations with attitudes of pure self-awareness, boosting creativity and enhancing emotional needs.

- Howlite enhances character building and a sense of inner cleanliness, which encourages behavior focused on decency and tact.
- It can also help calm emotions, slowing down overactive minds and help achieve deep, restful sleep.
- Howlite can help with the absorption of calcium in bones and teeth, and by balancing emotional needs, it also allows you to relax and release muscle tension due to great physical exertion or poor posture.

The soft and light properties of howlite make it a beautiful stone to pave the way for the receptivity of other stones or crystals used together. The howlite stone encourages our desire for knowledge undertaken and helps to maintain what has been learned while also allowing us to express it.

Jaietto

Jaietto is a mineral wood of coal, compact and very light, which has been immersed in water for millions of years, then compacted and fossilized.
The jaietto is not to be confused with Lignite which is a very young brown coal from organic material of vegetable origin, whose fossilization has not been completed.

- The jay is known for its powerful protective properties against evil spirits, spells and witchcraft, but also for its powerful qualities to increase the effectiveness of magic by Wiccan High Priestesses.
- Jet is an ideal stone for meditation and to increase spiritual awareness.
- Was used extensively in mourning jewelery in the Victorian era due to its dark color and modest appearance.
- The jaietto stone helps us to compensate for the aura of impure energies.

It can be used to cleanse and deprogram other crystals by placing them in a bowl with some smaller pieces of jet.
Those with nervousness and hyperactive individuals may find a calming benefit from jet, as it integrates higher vibrations into the lower chakras and brings a calming sense of wholeness to the individual.
Jaietto is known to work synergistically with moldavite.

Labradorite

Labradorite was discovered in the province of Labrador, Canada in 1770. A famous Eskimo legend tells that once upon a time the Northern Lights were actually imprisoned in the rock along the coast of Labrador. A wandering Eskimo warrior, with spear strokes, freed most of the lights trapped in the rock and those that remained formed labradorite. Highly mystical, Labradorite enhances innate intuition and enhances psychic abilities, making it ideal for working with the third eye chakra. Intuition and intellect are balanced by labradorite, allowing illusions to fade and true personal intentions to emerge.

- Labradorite is a crystal that manages to expand the limits of the conscious sphere, promoting a healthy re-evaluation of one's abilities and hidden talents.
- It can also help unite the subconscious with the conscious mind by expanding the limits of our mind.
- Labradorite can help with eye disorders, brain disorders, and help regulate metabolism and the digestive process.
- Excellent stone for those who suffer from panic attacks or have phobias.

Fun fact: Labradorite has been found in some meteorites.
The properties of labradorite make it an excellent stone for interpreting dreams and learning new ways to use them in everyday life. It is also very protective, it strengthens and protects the aura from energy losses by helping it to maintain a clean and balanced vibration, thus aligning the physical body with the etheric ones.

Apache Tear

The Apache Tear (obsidian tears apache) is a type of obsidian that is rough and opaque; it forms when hot lava immediately contacts cold air and solidifies rapidly before hitting the ground.
- Apache's Tear, a mineral produced by the energy of fire born in the depths of the earth, is a wonderful companion to work with Energy.
- Legend has it that Apache Tears are formed from the tears of Apache women over the deaths of their men. Apache Tears in crystal healing possess many of the qualities of Black Obsidian.

They are protective stones and are excellent to bring into contact with yourself or to use for meditation and your own spiritual path.

Lapis lazuli

Lapis lazuli is a semi-precious stone valued for its deep blue color while the many white streaks (of calcite) lower the value of lapis lazuli.

The Sumerians believed that lapis lazuli could hold the spirits of deities; in ancient Egypt, and more precisely, in "The Book of the Dead" it is stated that lapis lazuli in the shape of an eye could become an amulet of great power.

The Egyptians considered it, as shown in the Ebers Papyrus, to have medicinal properties for the eyesight.

Lapis lazuli is one of the stones in Aaron's "Armor of Judgment" as described in the Bible.

- The lapis lazuli stone helps us eliminate the old emotional baggage we carry around and which often hurts us, awakens intuition and increases the body's vibrational level.
- Excellent as a powerful defensive and protective stone (amulet) also for psychic attack blocks.
- Lapis lazuli reduces inflammation and pain (particularly in the head).
- Lapis lazuli is a stone that vibrates above all with the third eye chakra: it develops intuition by amplifying and expanding psychic and clairvoyant abilities.

Activates the pineal gland and opens communication with one's spiritual world, favoring the development of the imagination.
- Like most blue stones, lapis lazuli also stimulates and activates the throat chakra.

Being a strongly spiritual stone, it also vibrates with the fifth chakra, enhancing creativity, creating clarity in communication and depth of thought.

Precisely because lapis lazuli helps to develop depth of faith and great conviction, it increases self-confidence and understanding of one's spirituality, making one reach out towards the right decision; from this derives what is called "enlightenment", that is an instantaneous and surprising understanding of one's spiritual path.

Health-wise, lapis lazuli is linked to the well-being of the thyroid, throat, immune, respiratory and nervous systems.

It appears that wearing the mineral can relieve migraines and help those who feel anxious or depressed.

Larimar

The Larimar stone was discovered in the year 1916 in Barahona, southwest of the Dominican Republic. Discovered by a Spanish priest Miguel Domingo Fuertes, he reported the news but no mining action was taken.
There is only one mining location for this rare gem, and that is in the southwest corner of the country. Edgar Cayce (known photographer and clairvoyant) predicted that in one of the Caribbean islands, being the remains of the land of Atlantis, a blue stone of Atlantean origin would emerge with extraordinary healing attributes.

- The properties of the larimar make it a gem with enormous potential, one of the few crystals to balance all energy polarities.
- The larimar cools spirits and fears; calms and relieves stress and nourishes the physical and emotional body. The larimar can be a source of inspiration and encouragement towards the improvement of one's personal reality, especially on the spiritual and physical levels.
- It can relieve high blood pressure and stress-related problems, as well as relieve excess fever and inflammation. It can also be used to stimulate cartilage and to loosen annoying blockages in the head and neck.

The available quantity of larimar is still unknown, which makes the availability of this stone very uncertain in the long run. The larimar stone has the ability to decrease the frequency and intensity of hot flashes and when the kundalini energies have become uncomfortably active.

Magnetite

Magnetite is in crystallotherapy a stone indicated for the realization of desires: in fact, it attracts what one aspires to, both in terms of situations and people who are positive for the psyche.
- It is the mineral richest in iron and is above all famous for its magnetic force, often also polar-magnetic: precisely because of this property, it manages to balance the hemispheres of the brain very well, therefore it is considered excellent for keeping "feet firmly on the ground", as well as useful for being active and proactive.

This unusual mineral is very powerful in visualizing what you want and, above all, in attracting it to yourself, making it enter your life; the magnetism of these stones stimulates the achievement of abundance and prosperity and, last but not least, can also help to ensure that the maximum fruits are born from the love and commitment of an interpersonal relationship.
- The magnetic qualities of the stone allow one to have a more balanced vision of life, also helping to overcome emotional problems. For women suffering from premenstrual syndrome, magnetite is indicated to appease emotions and to reduce mood swings.
- It is a stone that increases our contact with the earth, therefore, it vibrates above all with the base chakra (at the base of the spine) and with the earth star chakra (located about 15 cm below the soles of the feet).
- It is an excellent remedy, therefore, to resort to if one embarks on a spiritual path. When used in meditation, it helps to enter the deepest states of concentration.

The connection with Mother Earth breeds a deeper appreciation of our planet, naturally increasing the ability to love it and to cherish.

It has a strong vibrational power: in the past magnetite was known as shamanic crystal; this is due to its strong ability to foster connection to nature, vibrating especially with the earth star chakra. Furthermore, its vibrations are very effective in helping to balance the whole aura.
• In this sense, it works well if two stones are used: one at the base of the spine, so that its energy is close to the base chakra, and the other on the top of the head, at the crown chakra. It is also normally used to bring the chakras and meridians into alignment.

By approaching the energy of nature through this stone, the whole organism is revitalized. For personal healing, hold a stone in each hand to balance both sides of the brain.
• Rebalances one's masculine and feminine part from a physical, emotional, mental and spiritual point of view: this balancing is very effective in improving one's cognitive and telepathic abilities.

Ultimately, magnetite can strengthen intuition especially in those who rely too much on rationality and logic: you can learn to trust your instincts and the flow of your sensations more, releasing all anxiety and negativity.
All this contributes to maintaining a meditative and relaxed state of mind.

Malachite

The properties of malachite are thought to be able to reach the innermost feelings of the person and reflect who one is, negative or positive.
In fact, malachite is called the "mirror stone of the soul". Malachite has been believed since ancient times to be a powerful protector of children, and it is believed to protect the wearer from accidents. It protects travelers and is of strong balance in relationships. Malachite powder was already used as early as 3000 BC. by the ancient Egyptians as a cosmetic for eye make-up.

- It is believed that looking at or wearing malachite can relax the nervous system and calm emotional disturbances, bringing a sense of peace and harmony.
- Malachite reminds us that we have a dual nature, and it is the duty of each person to know and govern their own person.
- To be used combined with copper to increase its power.

Mookaite

Mookaite has a strong connection with the energies of the Earth and its life force; this gem brings us into contact with the electromagnetic currents of the Earth and encourages us to combine the energies of both, providing stability to our life perspective and helping to make the right decisions based on objective knowledge.
Mookaite teaches us to raise the vibration of our bodies and thoughts so that we can dramatically slow down our aging process.
Give us a "young at heart" mentality and an ageless spirit.

- Traditionally, mookaite provides a powerful connection to the animal kingdom, strengthening instinct and our non-verbal communication with them.
- Also opens a powerful connection to our ancestors, bringing an intuitive understanding of the natural evolution of spirit.

Excellent stone for support to the reproductive system, to ease lower back tension, to strengthen the immune system, cleanse our liver and to fight the effects of aging. Mookaite is an excellent support during meditation, in particular it can be used to access the genetic memory to awaken all one's abilities.
It is an excellent balancer of the first chakras, and is able to greatly improve the flow of energy between the first three chakras, providing excellent grounding and discharge to the Earth.

Bull's Eye

It has the ability to greatly increase self-confidence and bring satisfaction, emotional comfort, and enhance artistry and talent, if innate.

The bull's-eye stone, with its intense vibrations, stimulates weak-willed people to express themselves fearlessly and courageously. It helps to defend oneself from oppressive situations and from people who don't know their place.

- Pain reliever, strengthens the solar plexus area and calms nervousness due to stress: useful to students for the help it gives to concentration.
- The bull's eye stone helps to center oneself, to consider the various points of view and to find one's inner point of balance between oneself and the world.

It is excellent in elixirs and to work in synergy with hawk's eye, sardonyx and hyaline quartz.

Hawk's Eye

Hawk's eye stone has always been traditionally associated with Ancient Egypt and more precisely with the eye of Horus. And right from Egypt it was believed to improve healing at a vibrational level and to pave the way for clearer communication between the perceptive part of the self and the physical part of our body, where the disease is actually manifested.
The hawk eye is also able to help visualize your spiritual dimension, better clarifying the personal sphere of material goals.

- Is also able to transform the material plans of the imagination into practical plans, thus allowing visions to be manifested concretely in the material world.
- Hawk's eye can improve circulation, bowel movements, coordinated use of legs and arms, and vision.
- May gently help tune the Third Eye and enhance psychic abilities such as clairvoyance.
- It helps us look at an emotional block that may be buried deep within our psyche.

The hawk eye is useful to anyone who undertakes shamanic journeys, astral journeys or spiritual challenges, as it is capable of connecting to ancestral entities or enlightened spirits who remain close to our dimension to offer guidance and support to those who ask for their help. Help.

Cat's Eye

Cat's Eye Stone is an excellent earth grounding stone that provides very high vibrational energy and effective etheric protection due to its ability to dissipate non-harmonic energies from our aura.
Cat's Eye works by amplifying the energies of other crystals, stimulating intuition and enhancing awareness, through increased creativity and kindness.
Greatly increases psychic abilities and the manifestation of material things. The cat's eye has always been believed, by mystics and esotericists, capable of giving deep philosophical thought and the ability to be wise.
It can be useful when greater concentration is needed or to stimulate healing. Traditionally believed to protect the wearer from evil spirits.
- Excellent stone for eye disorders, to improve night vision and to relieve headaches. It is also a mood regulator and is beneficial for eliminating tiredness and irritability.

It is believed to protect and multiply the wearer's wealth. For this purpose it is recommended to keep it in the same place where the money is kept.

Tiger's Eye

The stone called "tiger's eye" is a quartz crystal, with splendid bands of golden yellow color crossing it; it is a powerful mineral that helps harmony and balance, improving states of anxiety and fear.
It stimulates action and helps to make decisions with discernment and understanding, as well as with great mental clarity.
- The color ranges from yellow to brown and brown, crossed by beautiful striped shades.

The mineral is a great energy amplifier, as is the case with most quartz crystals, and will in turn increase the energy of any other crystals it is used with.
The stone combines the energy of the Earth with that of the Sun, keeping the rooting of the person who uses it strong, thus also revealing itself as an excellent meditation stone.
It enhances courage and tenacity, allowing these attributes to always be balanced with mental clarity and a joyful outlook.
The properties of the tiger's eye are also used to be able to discern the truth in every situation and to help understand the life one is living.
The benefits can help slow down the flow of energy through the body, which makes the gemstone very helpful for stress-related ailments.
- Excellent stone for arthritis and inflammation of bone tissue.
- It is said to be useful in cases of schizophrenia, various mental disorders and impulsive obsession.
- Promotes better energy flow through the body when worn.
- It thus becomes an excellent stone for concentration, especially for those with attention deficits.
- Tiger's Eye can be used to enhance psychic abilities and promote the activity of the third eye chakra.

It is suggested to use tiger's eye in combination with Hyaline Quartz, Serpentine and Moonstone.

This stone vibrates a lot with the sacral (or navel) chakra and gives a useful energy to improve creativity. Its vibration within this chakra also helps distracted or unwilling people to make commitments and carry them out, as it gives courage and fortitude.

- Since the tiger's eye binds to the ground through the base chakra, it helps to be calmer and more centered: in other words, it allows you to take the necessary steps to be more practical in life.

The tiger eye also stimulates the increase of Kundalini energy, the coiled snake that resides at the base of the spine. When stimulated, it can ascend through the spine: this process is said to lead to enlightenment.

If you want to use tiger eye for this purpose, you can combine serpentine with it, which in turn will facilitate the Kundalini awakening process..

White Onyx

Its name comes from the Greek word "onux", which means "nail". Legend has it that one day Cupid cut the divine nails of Venus with an arrowhead while she was sleeping and the Fates (the three daughters of Zeus who wove the thread of every man's destiny) immediately changed them into stone, so that no part of the divine body of Venus could ever be destroyed. The ancient Egyptians believed that white onyx could cool sexual ardor when overdone.

The properties of white onyx keep the memory of physical events surrounding a person. A strong stone to be used for psychic work as it tells the story of the wearer. A stone of strength, good for sportsmen or people under mental and emotional stress.

- The white stone brings balance to the mind and body, and is a wonderful stone for those who are fickle by nature, as it helps keep us grounded and focus our attention.

Traditionally it can be especially useful for skin conditions, infected wound healing, fungal infections, inflammation and even sunburn.

It helps to predict what lies beyond and to become the master of one's future, removing unnecessary dependencies on the growth process, especially unhealthy or annoying emotional and emotional involvements.

The white onyx elixir is excellent for our reddened skin or to revitalize it, to be used with repeated compresses during the day.

Opal

The opal contains the power of all the elements and their respective characteristics:
- The energy and strength of Fire.
- The prosperity, peace and well-being of the Earth.
- The intuition, emotions and sensitivity of Water.
- The communication and creativity of the Air.

The opal has a general beneficial effect on health, especially on the joints. It activates vital functions and helps the heart beat regularly and with serenity (especially the pink opal). Relieves digestive system disorders and balances the nervous system (especially the noble opal). Fire opal stimulates vital energy and is therefore useful for weak and apathetic people.

The opal inspires joie de vivre and stimulates the desire for change, therefore it is particularly suitable if important decisions have to be made. Promotes optimism and sexuality.

However, it is not a stone with an energy that is easy to manage: as it is closely connected with the planet Neptune and consecrated to truth and altruism, it is useless to try to use it if selfish or destructive purposes are pursued.

Especially, the fire opal is useful for depression and to strengthen the will.
- The fire opal variety acts on the 2nd chakra.
- The pink variety acts on the 4th chakra.
- The noble black variety and the chrysopal act on the 5th chakra.
- The noble white variety works on the 7th chakra.

The opal can be drained after use under running water.
To obtain visible effects on the spiritual level, it is advisable to carry the stone in close contact with the skin.

Boulder Opal

Boulder Opal is an excellent stone for progress, expansion and personal development. It helps connect our conscious with the subconscious, allowing for compensation and understanding of oneself on a psychic and mental level.
Boulder opal facilitates communication between our earthly dimension and that of other worlds of different dimensions. Precisely because of its deep connection with the earth, it becomes an excellent ally for our roots, especially during periods of substantial changes in our lives.
Allowing for emotional and mental balance, it soothes the inner soul and cleanses and brightens the personal aura, stimulating centering.
- It is used to access higher spirit guides and animal guides.
- Can be used to stabilize personal energy.
- Boulder opal is an excellent stone for the eyes and in communicating all forms of words.
- It is an emotional balancer that aids inner beauty and fidelity.

Wearing, touching and meditating with boulder opal helps to increase mental abilities such as creative visualization, intuition and clairvoyance, untapped potentials of the mind.
Boulder opal strengthens the will to live life to the fullest.

Opalite

Opalite ranges from light to milky in color, taking on an otherworldly light or luminous blue glow, especially when placed against a dark background.
That's why it is sometimes mistaken for moonstone.
It is also found in various shades of dark purple, lavender, and creamy white with swirls of yellow, tan, and dark brown and pink areas.
Its name comes from the Sanskrit word "Upala", which means precious stone.
Opalite is considered a healing stone, it removes energy blocks and helps fight fatigue. It also purifies the blood and kidneys.
Encourage you to explore yourself inside and all around, to discover that even the most unimaginable life goals can be achieved.

- It also relieves depression and decreases aggressive behavior.
- Opalite strongly attracts Beings of Light, it is a stone to be used in Angelic-type communication and to attract energies of Light towards environments.
- It is used in meditation, as it is associated with the third eye chakra and the crown chakra.
- Aids in interpreting psychic information and helps verbalize inner feelings.

Opalite can increase sex drive and enhance sexual experience. It is used in jewelry and by some adherents of Wicca and other pagan faiths in practices such as healing rituals.
Given the huge demand, it is possible to find artificial glass-based opalite as well.

Obsidian

Obsidian is a volcanic glass that forms following the rapid cooling of lava; it is found in various places in the world and in as many types, as well as in different colors.
Among the many shades, there is the rainbow-colored stone, with a colorful appearance with the presence of green, purple, brown and blue; another type is snowflake obsidian, which is a black and white stone. The latter has a strong spiritual vibration and psychic protection.
- Obsidian has the extraordinary and unnerving ability to dig deep into its own shadows, bringing forth great intuition and knowledge, both personal and about material things.
- It is an effective stone for combating stress and depression, the release of old grievances and acceptance of the past.
- Relieves pain and stimulates blood circulation.
- Furthermore, it is a protective stone against future problems: it can especially help those who, in some way, often get into trouble due to lack of judgment or personal inclination.

Minerals vibrate especially within the base chakra and help to get rid of excess energy through the earth chakra. In crystal therapy, obsidian helps spiritual communication, so much so that for centuries shamans have used these crystals to get in touch with their spirit guides. Furthermore, the mineral is known to amplify mediumistic powers and the gift of prophecy.
- By approaching this stone on the third eye, one can ask it what is the goal to be achieved in the current life.

Furthermore, it is also indicated to those who find it difficult to recognize the presence of problems, since it is a crystal that stimulates the search for truth and, therefore, its acceptance.

Black obsidian is not only a very beautiful stone, but also very easy to buy.

It is common to find jewels that, in addition to this element, also contain other nuances.

The dark stone is often used with other crystals to amplify its psychic protection aspect by combining it with black tourmaline, smoky quartz, shungite, fire agate, Libyan desert glass, brown tourmaline, stellerite, astrophyllite, golden rutilated quartz and tourmaline quartz.

Sunstone

The sunstone is also known by the name of heliolite, whose meaning derives from the Greek "helios" which means "sun" and from "lithos" which means "stone". The sunstone was used in Ancient Greece to represent the Sun God, Helios (or Apollo). In Greece the sunstone was believed to invigorate and improve the state of the physical body and spirit, bringing renewed health to both. This particular gemstone was prized by ancient wizards, who used the sunstone to attract the power of the sun by associating it with power and material wealth.

Sunstone properties are known for its powerful connection to light and the power of the sun, imparting a sunny character. It brings light to all situations, and is an optimal stone for the solar plexus chakra and all chakras.

It is a powerful stone to dispel fears and phobias of all kinds, it increases willpower, as well as personal vital energy; It can provide the stamina and energy needed to undertake projects and activities that may encounter objective obstacles.

- Excellent for the chronicity of sore throats and to relieve the pain of gastric ulcers.
- Also used for cartilage, rheumatism and general aches.
- Brought in close contact, it stimulates the personal power of attraction.

The properties of the stone of the sun are enhanced if used together with the moonstone, especially in solstices, in personal rituals, in energy works and spells. Together they represent the balance of power between physical characteristics and psychic and spiritual characteristics.

Moonstone

Moonstone has been used for centuries in a variety of cultures. Being a perfect expression of yin energy, i.e. the mysterious and placid energy of the moon, this stone is in turn the bearer of calm, peace and balance.
The serenity and tranquility that the mineral generates has a sensual and extraordinary effect, infusing creativity and optimism with its soft glow. Anciently, but still today, moonstone is considered a sacred stone in India.
Associated with the moon, the stone was worn by the goddess Diana and in the East moonstone amulets were often hung on fruit trees to ensure fertile and abundant crops and in the Middle Ages, by alchemists, it was believed that if held in the mouth, the stone di luna could help make appropriate decisions.
- Moonstone is a gem of intuition and deep understanding, it helps balance the emotional body by accentuating freedom of expression and particularly attenuates aggressive tendencies.
- Bringing feminine energy, moonstone opens up our more yin side, can stimulate pineal gland functioning, balance internal hormonal cycles with the rhythms of nature, relieve menstrual and pregnancy pain, promote fertility and help stimulate the lymphatic and immune system.
- May reduce swelling and excess body fluid.

The finest moonstone is mainly mined from Sri Lanka.
The ideal and most resonant time to use moonstone is during the full moon phase; moreover, thanks to its association with water, it appears to be very protective of people who live near seaside places.
- Moonstone connects the second and sixth chakras beautifully to each other, enhancing intuitive sensitivity through behaviors that are less overwhelmed by personal feelings.

- Works wonders when paired with garnet, (revealing the truth behind our illusions) and when used in conjunction with amethyst in the higher chakras.
- Moonstone is a very personal gem: it reflects the soul of the person who owns it. It does not take away or add anything to the personality, but shows it as it really is: this is why it is useful during meditation.

It is excellent for women, but can be indicated to men to encourage them to express their emotions. The gem is therefore used to stimulate the functioning of the pineal gland and the balance of internal hormonal cycles, adapting them to the rhythms of nature

In feng shui, moonstone is used for its calming properties, its yin energy and the fact that it recalls the element of water. A home or office with too much yang energy can benefit from the compensation that the stone will be able to generate. Make sure you take the best care of your moonstone, whether it's spheres and ovals, or jewelry.

Clean it often and gently, trying to preserve it from exposure to strong sunlight.

Pyrite

Pyrite, given its resemblance to gold, has made it a strong traditional symbol in all latitudes and cultures of the world to attract money and good luck.
Furthermore, pyrite symbolizes the warmth and the vital and lasting presence of the sun, favoring the recall of beautiful memories of love and friendship.

- It has the ability to capture earth and fire energies, making it an excellent tool for both balancing the root chakra and balancing and strengthening the aura.
- Pyrite can help by giving a feeling of increased vitality during times of hard work or increased stress. Pyrite can increase physical stamina, stimulate the intellect and help transform thought into intelligent action.
- Strongly recommended for people who grapple with big conceptual ideas on a daily basis, whether in business, the arts, or education.

Its properties strengthen mental abilities and awareness of higher forms of knowledge.
It can improve communication skills by driving away anxiety and frustration. Creative and intuitive impulses can be more stimulated when used together with fluorite and calcite.

Citrine Quartz

Almost all the citrine that is available on the market today is actually the amethyst stone (the one of the least value and beauty) which undergoes a high heat treatment. Natural citrine ranges from a pale yellow to a more intense yellow; anything that is dark orange, brown, to reddish brown has been heat treated.
The only exception to this is the darker citrine Citrine Madeira, so named due to the similarity of color to Madeira wines. It is a stone that in ancient times was used as protection against poisons and psychic disorders.
- Citrine enhances the healing energy of the physical body and opens the conscious mind to intuition. An energizing crystal, invigorating against chronic fatigue and highly beneficial, it also increases internal motivation and promotes physical activity, which in turn improves digestion and helps cleanse organs.
- It can also work as a blood detoxifier.
- Develops inner calm and confidence and makes us less sensitive and more open to constructive criticism. It can dispel negative feelings and help us accept the flow of events. Citrine can eliminate self-harming behaviors or tendencies and increase self-esteem.

It is also known as a "success" stone because it is capable of promoting personal success and abundance, especially in the world of business and commerce.
Citrine can increase one's optimism in any situation, bringing a more positive outlook into the subconscious mind, allowing one to get into the flow of things with better results.

Smoky Quartz

Smoky quartz gets its color from natural sources of radioactivity, which are close to where quartz crystals form.
In Traditional Chinese Medicine, smoky quartz is used to stimulate the meridians, and in ancient India, yogis have always kept it close to raise the Kundalini.
The Romans used smoky quartz as a stone of deep mourning, which allowed them to better overcome the pain generated.
If the stone is natural, (given the enormous requests, today it is artificially treated with radiation) the smoky quartz is a stone with a strong transformation power and is often used for the removal of negativity and non-harmonic energies in places, given its transformation capacity.

- Enhances survival instinct, aids physical body acceptance and sexual nature, and stimulates the base chakras so energy can flow naturally.
- May be helpful for all kinds of problems related to the lower torso, reproductive organs, menstrual cramps, fertility problems.
- Helps regulate body fluids and fluid retention.
- Smoky Quartz is an excellent stone for energy workers who are in contact with other people.

Its properties make it an excellent choice for those who are used to physical contact with others and with their inner self. It is able to repel an enormous amount of disharmonious energy from different sources, making it particularly excellent to use for one's psychic protection.

Hyaline Quartz

Hyaline quartz is also called rock crystal, which derives from the Greek word krustallos which means ice, due to the belief that rock crystal was formed from ice. It is the most widespread mineral on earth and is formed in all environments and all types of rock, and has been known for a very long time.
Clear Quartz is the most versatile and powerful healing stone of all crystals, able to work on any condition. Remarkable is its ability to amplify the subtle energies around it, including those of all other crystals.
- Greatly strengthens the aura, and is used to activate and align all chakras, even the transpersonal chakras.
- Rock crystal provides more energy, and stimulates the immune system to prevent serious diseases.
- Facilitates heart function, prevents heart attack, carries oxygen to the brain and stabilizes blood pressure.

In meditation it strengthens one's energy field and when used together with hematite it facilitates grounding and rooting. It also allows for emotional clarity and purity of heart, amplifying spiritual insights.
Generates electromagnetism and dissipates static electricity.
If hyaline quartz is combined with lepidolite, amber and tourmaline, it facilitates their functions.
Given its hardness (7 out of 10 on the Mohs scale) and the enormous worldwide demands, it is very likely to find glass objects (spheres, skulls, lasers and more) instead of quartz.

Rose Quartz

The rose quartz stone was found in the area once known as Mesopotamia (present day Iraq) with pieces dating back to 6000 BC.
Rose Quartz works closely with the Heart chakra, and, in fact, is called "the Stone of the Heart": it represents love, beauty, peace, and forgiveness. It is a sweet, gentle stone, a calming stone that warms the center of our heart. It is able to balance our emotions, thus giving inner peace and harmony.

- Rose quartz energy is among the most relaxing and promotes empathy, reconciliation and forgiveness of others.

It is able to reduce stress and tension in the heart, eliminate anger, jealousy and resentment in others, relieving heart problems and discomfort associated with holding such negative emotions in us.

- Rose Quartz can also be used to balance all chakras and to remove inharmonious energy and replace it with love energy. He is capable of aligning the mental, emotional and astral bodies on his own, which is why it is always useful to carry stones or wear some jewellery.

A quick way to benefit from the sensual and loving virtues of rose quartz is to drink a spring water elixir with the essence of the stone.
Furthermore, to promote a calm and harmonious environment where we live, it is very advisable to have at least one piece or several pieces scattered in strategic places, such as desks, bedside tables or shelves.

Rutilated Quartz

Rutilated quartz is a type of quartz that contains rutile (titanium dioxide) in needle form. Rutile needles can be reddish, or they can be golden, silver, or on very rare occasions, greenish in color. The inclusions of rutilated quartz have been called Venus hair since the Middle Ages, and from that period the belief that the stone can slow down the aging process was born.

- Rutilated quartz is a stone that has both the energetic vibration energy of clear quartz and the amplifying power of rutile, which makes it very useful when combined with other stones, especially labradorite, citrine and chalcopyrite.

The properties of rutilated quartz make it an illuminator for the soul, a stone to promote spiritual growth. The stone is known to be an energizing stone that helps in gaining and releasing energy on all levels.
- It is said that it can also alleviate imposed loneliness and alleviate the guilt feelings generated by others, thus making happiness possible.
- It can increase one's autonomy and self-esteem by instilling the ability to find one's own path.
- It is a useful stone for eating disorders, and the absorption of nutrients from food, tissue regeneration, fatigue, and depression.

It is used for meditation, spiritual communications, and lucid dream work. Stone particularly suitable for the search for greater spiritual experiences and meditation on feminine energies.

Tourmalinate Quartz

Tourmalinate quartz is formed through the combination of tourmaline and clear quartz (or rock crystal) at very high temperatures and pressures, when both minerals are in a liquid state and therefore able to mix with each other.
Tourmaline Quartz is commonly used in rituals as a powerful symbol of unity, being a stone of high stabilizing energy, it is also used to increase personal power. A particular property is that of returning to the sender particular energies that are not harmonic or synergistic with one's own.
This effect, with appropriate programming, is very similar to a spell, a mirror effect, and allows the auric field to always be shielded and protected from any negativity.

- It can be useful for relieving work stress, and the resulting nervous tension.
- It can also be used to solve seemingly unsolvable problems and helps us to think with mental clarity by promoting a relaxed attitude.
- Tourmaline quartz can help treat digestive tract disorders and detoxify the whole body; it can be used as an aid for those who are trying to detox and cleanse their bodies after substance abuse or for those who are looking to improve their diet or nutrition.

Tourmaline quartz is particularly effective on the secondary chakras of the hands and feet, and works very well and in synergy with the properties of charoite, obsidian, jet and citrine.

Rhodochrosite

Rhodochrosite is also known as the Inca Rose Stone, and is an excellent conductor of energy; in all the Indian peoples of South America, this stone is a symbol of divine protection that has more value than gold.
Rhodochrosite has a very toning quality for the heart and skin but it is one of the most important stones of the solar plexus chakra, as it manages to move stagnant energy allowing physical and emotional communication.
It is of an intense pink color with red shades; transparent crystals, similar to pink tourmaline, of a raspberry red color have rarely been found.
- The darker variety has a good effect on the 1st chakra: it must therefore be placed on the back, at the base of the spine and from there the vibrations will reach the kidneys and pancreas.
- Light rhodochrosite has an action on the 4th chakra and has proved to be of great help for those who suffer from very strong personalities, depending on them to the point of totally undergoing the will of others. It is, therefore, one of the most useful stones in relieving and overcoming all forms of abuse and emotional trauma.

On the physical side, it helps the spleen, kidneys and heart, the pituitary gland and blood circulation; promotes eye health. The high manganese content makes it a good general tonic for the body. Strengthens the immune system, acts positively on the activity of the ovaries and testicles, fights sterility and impotence, reduces typical menopausal and climacteric disorders.
For a soothing bath, add a piece of rhodochrosite to the bath water or wear the stone while bathing.

Rhodonite

Rhodonite is a gem that gives self-confidence starting from trust in one's heart, encouraging responsibility, generosity and cooperation between individuals and the community.
- Confers the potential for quick learning and personal development, helping to express trust and loving kindness on the physical plane on a day to day basis with those around us, always instilling calm and constantly nourishing the soul through heart and love.

Rhodonite encourages people to find ways of being of service to humanity and helps draw synchronicities into this goal. It can enhance power in those with truly altruistic intentions.
- Excellent stone for detoxification and purification of the liver, for the nervous system and to reduce swelling and inflammation of the eyes.
- Finds great employment when associated with businesses such as musicians, peaceworkers, lightworkers, and those in the service-to-others industry, given its enormous potential to maintain harmony and rhythm.

Rhodonite is a stone that finds empathy in working with prehnite, rose quartz and galena.

Ruby

The ruby has always been a stone linked to nobility, so much so that it is considered the most magnificent of all gems; the ancients believed it was more precious than the other minerals, even more so than the diamond. Revered in multiple cultures throughout history, the ruby has always been seen as a talisman of passion, protection and prosperity; it symbolizes the sun and its bright color is similar to an unquenchable flame.
This beautiful crystal emits a pure red ray, with a vitality unmatched in the mineral kingdom.
- Actively stimulates the base chakra, or first chakra, increasing vitality and "Ki", the life force energy, throughout the body and spirit.
- Promotes mental clarity, concentration and motivation and gives a sense of power to the wearer, with a self-confidence and determination that overcome shyness and push to dare.

The mineral encourages sensual pleasure, stimulates the heart and improves blood circulation.
- By increasing one's sexual desire, it can be used to activate the Kundalini. It has always been associated with passionate love and, in ancient times, it was considered a suitable wedding stone.

Ruby is a red corundum, an aluminum oxide mineral with chromium inclusions, responsible for its bright colour. The hue varies depending on where it is extracted and can show pinkish, orange, purple or even wine-colored hues.
All natural rubies have imperfections within them, including color impurities and Rutile needle inclusions, which give rise to the "shiny silk" effect.

The star ruby variety has the same metaphysical properties as the ruby, but with greater healing power and magical energies; it is most powerful at a full moon. It is extremely effective in cases of self-harming people, with erotic problems and with traumas of a sexual nature.

Wearing a ruby, or carrying it with you, helps overcome tiredness and lethargy. Stimulates circulation, to regenerate the body's vitality and energy. Those who are highly nervous or irritable, however, may find this stone hyper-stimulating, thus seeing their hyperactivity increased.
- Considered a blood-related mineral, it strengthens the heart, myocardium, ventricles and coronary arteries, stimulating blood circulation. It also regulates the menstrual cycle and relieves related discomfort. Furthermore, it is indicated to detoxify the body, blood and lymph, thus helping to fight fever and infections.

Stimulates the kidneys and spleen and counteracts swelling in the legs and feet. It can also help in weight regulation when it increases due to nervous hunger. Ruby is an aphrodisiac and allows one to experience all forms of love, ranging from wild sensuality to mystical communion.
- The intense energy of the ruby sharpens the mind, bringing greater awareness and excellent concentration.
- Promotes a courageous attitude and can increase one's success during argumentative discussions or controversies.
- It also protects those sensitive natures who lack self-esteem, overcoming the fear of not being beautiful or lovable.

It is purified and recharged on a rock crystal druze. Instead, it is better to avoid direct sunlight, which could discolor it.

Selenite

Selenite contains a lot of feminine energy and is often used to connect and communicate with the Divine; in the past it was often used as a magic wand to facilitate the conveyance of one's intentions for the Higher Self or the Universe.
Selenite is the stone of tranquility, it gives a very high vibration, and is capable of instilling mental clarity and a deep sense of inner peace, providing flexibility to our nature and strength for our important decisions.
- It is a stone that goes well with intense spiritual work, especially in meditation, as well as being a powerful crystal of psychic communication.
- Can assist in communication in the past tense with ancestors and spirit guides.
- Selenite also has the wonderful property of being able to energetically purify and cleanse other crystals of heavy energies.
- Can help at the cellular level, spine and skeletal system, is used to improve skin tone and the body's ability to absorb calcium.

Ancient popular beliefs, but common all over our planet, have also emphasized the use of selenite to increase libido. The properties of selenite are often used in magic to evoke protection from the realm of the dead and to also dispel negative energy in environments.
Excellent reveals itself in esotericism if used on special grids, or around the house or in the corners of a room (together with the salt, but without touching), to create a safe and peaceful space.

Seraphinite

The name seraphinite comes from the Latin word "Seraphin", referring to the first order of Angels. The allusion to the Angels is due to the mica present in the stone which recalls the feathery appearance of the wings of the Angels.
Seraphinite is highly sought after in the world of metaphysics and mineral collecting.
It can be used to cleanse and purify the space around us.
Particular in the work on the chakras since it has the ability to align and balance them all.
- Excellent for cleaning the Aura.
- Serafinite is an earthly and ethereal stone at the same time and allows us to obtain more understandable divine messages and to perceive the unconditional love of the Beings of Light.

It can suggest to us the knowledge and understanding that hidden mysteries can be known.

Serpentine

It is a stone considered important and magical for the Assyrians, already in 4000 BC. it was used and known as Za-tu-mush-gir. Serpentine is the stone from which the tablet of chapter 30 of the Egyptian Book of the Dead was made.
The Aztecs value all green stones and serpentine was used to grace the interior of their temples, as well as in China and India where it is often incorporated into altars, sculptures and temple decorations.
Serpentine is also present on the breastplate of Aaron, brother of Moses, in Exodus (there were 12 stones on the breastplate and they represented the 12 tribes).
- It's a powerful stone of protection and can be used to eliminate energy blocks in all chakras but above all to help regenerate and strengthen the heart chakra. In fact, serpentine is an energetically powerful healing stone that aids in the clearing of blocked areas, bringing the chakras back into balance.
- The synergy with jade, chrysoprase and seraphim is excellent.

Carrying serpentine with you will help you relax your human nature, as well as being an excellent stone for meditation. It is useful for those who are dedicated and helping others to access the primary energy of our planet and to heal the earth. Serpentine can be used for Kundalini rising - it stimulates the natural upward path and can decrease the discomfort that is sometimes associated with Kundalini energy practices.

Shiva Lingam

The Shiva Lingam, which is a blend of agate, basalt and jasper in quartz, is considered a devotional symbol of the Lord Shiva. The egg shape is considered a phallic symbol of Shiva, the famous Hindu god; legend says that the Shiva Lingam compound comes from a meteorite that crashed into the earth millions of years ago; the currents of the Narmada River helped shape the stone into an egg shape.

- The shiva lingam represents both the masculine force (Knowledge) and the feminine force (Wisdom), as well as the Cosmic Egg from which all creation emerged.
- Shiva lingam is to feed the entire chakra system, increase strength and enhance vitality, stimulates kundalini energy bringing about positive change and aiding our personal growth.
- It is a powerful symbol of love: it opens our path towards true love which leads to unity.

The stone is able to balance all the energies of the physical body, for infertility and impotence problems (especially male), and is recognized as an excellent stone for rooting. It possesses a supreme ability to amplify the life force (Ki) and vibrational power of other stones or crystals, and is a stone that does not require recharging or cleansing.

Together with Moldavite, it can bring great transformation and protection into our lives, encouraging both to break free from old patterns and to embrace new ideas and changes..

Shungite

Shungite is found only in Russia, in Karelia, in the area of Lake Onega; scientists estimate the age of shungite around 2 billion years, when there were no life forms on Earth. And the fact that Shungite contains fullerene molecules (elementary carbon atoms arranged in a unique molecular context in nature) which are present in very minute quantities in nature, and how they are found present in the mineral still remains a mystery. Shungite is called the "Stone of Life" due to its antibacterial properties.

- It is also considered for its properties of eliminating and absorbing all that is a danger on people and living beings, and of concentration and restoration for all that is useful for a human being, and also for shielding electromagnetic radiation harmful of any origin, even radioactive.
- This unusual rock has a profound positive action, and is a stone of rejuvenation.
- Shungite will help people adjust to the new frequencies present on earth, allowing many to ascend to the higher realms of existence.

Shungite's antibacterial properties make it a stone of power and healing, highly effective for grounding and useful for calming emotions and reducing mood swings.
The stone maintains the youth and beauty of the skin and makes the hair stronger, adding shine and silkiness.
Today it is used worldwide by geobiologists to balance geopathies and dissipate emotional energy.

Emerald

Emerald stones are among the most appreciated: the green energy, which vibrates with the heart chakra, makes the mineral the stone of success and abundance.
- To encourage the removal of negativity, tradition has it that natural emerald crystals are able to stimulate positive actions and results, providing the strength to overcome any problems in life.

The light green color is present in nature in grass, plants and trees, which give off the energy just mentioned; the force of nature is always enclosed in green minerals, exactly as in the case of the emerald.
This stone also has many excellent qualities and is usually associated with those born in the month of May.
Emeralds are a variety of beryl: very popular for jewellery, they come mostly from India, Russia, Zimbabwe, Africa, Egypt, Austria, Brazil and Colombia. The green ray of these beautiful stones encourages you to have respect for all life forms and for all of creation, living with more love.
- All emerald specimens emit this energy and have a strong effect on the deepest emotions.

Feelings such as compassion, hope, loyalty, reassurance, kindness, benevolence, goodness and unconditional love are connected to a cosmic and spiritual form of love, which embraces every living thing. For those who believe in the potential of stones and crystal healing, all people are "Divine Beings in a physical body". Yet many feel blocks in living a life full and characterized by love.
Stress leads to brooding over one's misfortunes every day; meditating with the emerald can help you improve, rediscovering yourself full of love for yourself and for others.

Additionally, these stones can soothe negative emotions and create positive vibes, to help us break through the psychological obstacles that block energetic potentials.
- Emerald is also used to relieve stress, improve memory and facilitate understanding. It can also stimulate economic abundance. A new prosperity at all levels can be the natural result of being accompanied by the emerald and its energy.

Carrying an emerald in your pocket during the day and keeping it under your pillow at night can already be very useful, not to mention that jewels with emerald stones or gems are all very beautiful and elegant. The longer the emerald is kept in one's aura, the more benefits it can produce within the wearer.
- Emerald can be combined with other varieties of beryl, such as aquamarine and goshenite.

Moreover:
- Pale green hyddenite has a strong energy that combines well with emerald to aid in emotional healing. For this purpose, other stones that can be combined are green apophyllite, pink rhodochrosite, rhodonite and lilac lepidolite.

Among the stones that can be used with the emerald, there are others that vibrate with the heart chakra, such as dioptase, green aventurine, green amethyst, variscite and moldavite. Again, pink kunzite, pink quartz and pink morganite of the same color.

Sodalite

Sodalite was originally discovered in Greenland in 1811 and got its name from its high sodium content.
- Known as the stone of logic, rationality and efficiency, sodalite is a stone of profound truth and brings this into all aspects of life.

Sodalite works with the Throat and Third Eye Chakras, combining these energies in ways that promote rational thought, purpose, companionship, and trust in others, generating general well-being inspired by truth, idealism, and from objectivity.
- The properties of sodalite therefore make it an excellent meditative stone that opens up our spiritual awareness, combining our logic with our intuition.
- Sodalite can reduce high blood pressure, it is also associated with the thyroid, giving a calming and regulating effect on the gland, on the neuro-vegetative system and on all glandular functions.

By balancing the endocrine system, it also strengthens the metabolism. It promotes restful sleep, it is also useful for the vocal cords, larynx, hoarseness and throat.
It can be used in group work where cooperation and mutual trust is needed.
- Sodalite is an excellent stone for alleviating our fears, phobias and other-induced guilt, and is appropriate for anything that may hinder our healthy growth.

If you work in a group, this stone cements and coordinates the team's actions and objectives. In fact, develop harmony, trust and willpower, improving the sharing of programs and objectives to be achieved. Sodalite is also an excellent stone for communication: this action is especially strong at the level of the throat chakra. It encourages rational and intuitive thinking, to verbally communicate one's thoughts in a calm and relaxed

way, maintaining good clarity of the concepts one wishes to express. To accentuate the feeling of mental clarity, it can be combined with honey-colored calcite.
- If you have to speak in public, the stone promotes calm and balance, increasing self-esteem and keeping panic attacks away. Precisely because it acts above all at the level of the third eye and throat chakra, it is important to wear it in the form of earrings or necklaces, in order to maintain its influence in these areas.

Sugillite

Sugillite owes its name to the Japanese geologist who discovered the first specimens, Ken-ichi Sugi.
- It is a particular stone, considered one of the stones of love and one of the most important for the fourth chakra.
- Represents spiritual love and wisdom, and is capable of aligning all chakras allowing Kundalini energy to be opened and directed throughout the body.

Wearing or carrying Sugilite with you increases the search for freedom, drawing inspiration and trust. Excellent for movement disorders and epilepsy.

Sugillite is a stone widely used to recall visions and to stimulate our third eye, allowing visionary experience and higher perceptions.
- It is a stone that favors rest and inner calm.
- Brings us to balance left brain function and helps anyone integrate into the world or a new environment.

Together with the amethyst, it amplifies the protective power of our aura.

Iron Tiger

The Iron Tiger is a gemstone composed of red jasper, hematite and tiger's eye that fused together over two billion years as tectonic plates shifted to create the continent of Australia.
- Literally embodies the growth and evolution of Mother Earth. The properties of the iron tiger are of enormous grounding and powerful protection, especially protection from sudden dangers.

The Iron Tiger is also a strong stone of clarity and self-knowledge, as it makes energy available and accessible to allow truth to be seen beneath the surface of apparent problems.
- It is of great help and support in balancing the three lower chakras: it connects them allowing for the expression of passion and imagination, also aiding in creative endeavors and all types of artistic and visual skills.
- The Iron Tiger has the ability to greatly increase self-confidence and bring satisfaction, emotional comfort and enhance artistry and talent, if innate.
- Its properties can improve resistance and it is particularly useful for people whose daily life requires excessive physical effort.

Calming for emotional integrity and self-centering, Iron Tiger is said to balance red and white blood cells, improve muscle structure, aid the liver and nervous system. It can help those with strong chemical or noise sensitivity.

Topaz

Topaz is a crystal related to truth and the ability to forgive. It is a symbol of chastity, happiness, true friendship and hope. It helps the wearer to find their purpose in life, to be more aware of their thoughts, feelings and actions and, last but not least, their karmic effects. In this way, topaz is able to activate our cosmic awareness.

- By removing stagnant energies, it directs the body's strength to those places where it is needed most and helps release tension, promoting feelings of joy and happiness. The mineral's healing abilities are related to physical and spiritual renewal.

Topaz in its purest form is transparent, but rarely in this form is it available in nature. The impurities present within the crystalline lattice are responsible for the different colors of the stone.

Topaz crystals are usually yellow, but can also be white, gray, gold, green, blue, pink, brown, clear, or semi-transparent. When irradiated, topaz can go from light shades to darker and more intense colors.

The golden yellow variety of topaz is known as imperial topaz, while the clear one is usually called white topaz.

- Topaz is one of the twelve stones in the breastplate of the ancient Jewish high priests, as mentioned in the book of Exodus.
- The stones on the breastplate, along with 12 powerful angels, are believed to protect the gate to Heaven.
- The stone helps maintain a practical point of view in facing life, aiming for the most effective solutions to any problem or situation, without wasting time. The crystal can also be indicated in daily meditation and visualization.

- It can open the doors to universal energy and give courage, will and strength to make the necessary changes to one's existence.

Topaz crystal, especially if of high purity and transparency, is a vector of solar and masculine energy: for this reason it can open and balance a certain number of chakras. Powerful to strengthen the entire body, it balances, soothes and purifies emotions and thoughts, releasing stress and bringing joy. From a spiritual point of view, this stone gives love and peace.

As a healing element, it promotes rejuvenation and improves endocrine problems or related to asthma and thrombosis.

Imperial Topaz

The intense golden yellow topaz, as already mentioned, is called "imperial topaz".
For the Hindu community, wearing this mineral close to the heart bestows long life, beauty and intelligence. The ancient Egyptians believed that yellow topaz protected against all negativity, associating the color yellow with the sun god Ra. Similarly, the Romans always connected the mineral to the sun. The ancient Greeks used it when they needed to restore their strength and to guarantee themselves protection: they were, in fact, convinced it could bring them closer to the divinities.
- The crystal is believed to be extremely energizing, being a warm stone. Promotes creativity, and brings a sense of trust and protection. Free from stale and negative energies, fatigue and tension.

Finally, some believe that imperial topaz is useful for preventing fire theft.
Last but not least, it would be effective in case of insomnia, depression and panic attacks, as it gives a positive and optimistic attitude.
Finally, strengthen the flow of energy, protect the heart, improve blood circulation, relieve pain from rheumatoid arthritis, protect the kidneys, liver and endocrine glands.

Tourmaline

The name of tourmaline comes from the Sinhalese word "Thuramali" or "Thoramalli" which translates as "stone of mixed colors". Metaphysically, tourmaline (there are various colors) is one of the most powerful stones to work with.
- Tourmaline provides a balance of masculine/feminine energies within our bodies, and is excellent for balancing the hemispheres of the brain.
- It is a powerful vibrational regulator that helps maintain, stimulate and purify our energy centers in the body.

It is well known that tourmaline is a purification stone that has the power to divert and transform negative energy, (especially that generated by electric and magnetic fields and radiation), and is, therefore, very protective and widely used as a healing stone. grounding.
- Tourmaline is able to improve one's awareness, increase self-esteem and amplify one's psychic energies.

Excellent for concentration and communication, but also useful in relaxing the physical body and the mind crowded with too many thoughts.
- It is also used as a purifier for our aura, and is an excellent stone for dispelling fears, obsessions and neuroses, bringing freshness and emotional stability.

Tourmaline is particularly suitable in periods of extreme stress, and it is the crystal that must not be missed by those who work with crystal therapy and for those who are, for work reasons, in close contact, even physically, with other people.

Turquoise

Turquoise has been used for thousands of years, so much so that it is one of the oldest stones for making jewellery; in crystallotherapy it has remarkable metaphysical properties connected to the "ether" element.
The natural energy of these stones helps communicate truth, as turquoise increases spiritual strength and the ability to express oneself. Not surprisingly, it vibrates a lot with the throat chakra and can help manifest clairvoyant abilities, as well as balance the male and female aspects.
- In addition to vibrating with the throat chakra, turquoise also vibrates with the third eye chakra, which allows you to access greater self-awareness: this can be useful if you intend to work on your psychic sphere to better communicate this that feels spiritual.

Turquoise generally comes from Australia, Iran, Afghanistan, Tibet and the southwestern part of the United States; it can also be found in France, Great Britain, Russia, Poland, Egypt, China, Peru and Mexico.
- The mineral is a hydrated aluminum and copper phosphate, its most common color is blue. However, the stone also exists in other variations, such as green, white and purple. Generally turquoise stones are blue when copper is also present, while they are green when there are elements of iron.
- When none of these minerals are present, very rare forms of white turquoise occur.

This stone especially resonates with the throat chakra, helping to communicate truth, with wisdom and absolute sincerity. If you are shy, turquoise can help you launch more into conversations, therefore, be more confident when speaking, as well as develop a certain calm and tranquility for public interactions.

The mineral also vibrates strongly with the heart chakra: this increases empathy, makes you more compassionate and facilitates forgiveness. Thus, it ensures that energy flows through love for the world.
- Being a stone with strong spiritual value, it's very useful for stress, as well as preventing mood swings.
- It has been known since ancient times to be a protective stone, so you can relax during meditation with turquoise, as it will act as a shield against any negativity. Also, its vibration can help in meditative forms that are aimed at exploring past lives.
- Furthermore, it can also stimulate energies by working with the sacral chakra and the navel chakra: in this way it improves creativity and the ability to solve problems.

In light of all this, wearing earrings made with turquoise is useful if you are working on developing your psychic powers, by making the stone itself resonate with the third eye and throat chakra. Instead, if you want to develop greater empathy and a stronger ability to love, or if you want to feel more protected from negativity, a necklace holds the mineral closer to the heart chakra.

Turchesite

Turquoise stone is not turquoise itself but its turquoise powder or paste.
Legend has it that if worn it brings protection against lightning, and in the East it is believed that looking at turquoisesite in the early morning makes the day pleasant and without unexpected events.
- Turquoise is a stone of purification, dispels negative energy and can be worn for protection against external influences or pollutants in the atmosphere. It is capable of stabilizing mood swings and instilling inner calm.

It helps the absorption of nutrients, strengthens the immune system, contains the anti-inflammatory and detoxification effects and viral infections.
As a stone of communication, turquoise opens the benevolent connections between friendship and love, allowing greater clarity and understanding between the two feelings.
It also allows you to strengthen your convictions, courage and personal charisma.
- The notoriety of turquoise is due to its properties widely used in the treatment of depression, promoting the inner strength possessed to get out of the crisis.
- It is also a good stone for self-realization and deep meditations.
- If used for crystal therapy, it should be discharged and charged once a month, and its properties are amplified when combined with hematite and rock crystal.

Not to be exposed to strong sunlight.

Unakite

Unakite stone gets its name from the Greek word "epidosis" which means "to grow together". This name is due to the fact that unakite is the result of three minerals together: feldspar, epidote and quartz, and it is precisely through these materials joined together that unakite conveys its particular message.

It is a stone that balances our emotional and spiritual bodies, providing us with an extremely gentle release of our energy blockages anchored in the solar plexus.

- It keeps our spirits up when we're feeling low or easily conditioned, never letting us lose sight of the beauty in life.
- It is useful for the reproductive system, for healthy pregnancies and for the healthy and harmonious development of unborn children.
- Also used during recovery from major trauma, it helps us by prompting our body to remember the state of perfect health.
- Carrying it will help us maintain a healthy balance between the spiritual and mundane lives, allowing them to communicate in order to help us create the life we need.

The combination with the moonstone is excellent, the unakite helps to keep the connection between the lower chakras and the upper chakras firmly through the heart chakra.

Sapphire

Sapphire, in all its celestial hues, is a stone of wisdom, kingship, prophecy, and divine favor. Its blue color brings order and healing to the mind, giving strength and alertness, as well as the ability to see beyond superficial appearances, using deeper knowledge.
- Stimulates the throat and third eye chakras, allowing access to deeper levels of consciousness in order to gain greater self-understanding.

Associated with the planet Saturn, in crystal therapy it improves self-discipline and helps to materialize the goals that have been set. The mineral is a variety of corundum, which is an aluminum oxide.

Blue is considered the primary color of sapphire, although it can actually be found in many other shades. It is thought that the current lapis lazuli in the past were referred to as sapphires. However, all sapphires are stones of wisdom, individual colors add different shades to it.

- Black Sapphire: leads to trust in one's intuition and wisdom. It protects, relieves anxiety and pain and is a useful talisman when looking for work.
- Green Sapphire: brings wisdom, fidelity and integrity. Encourage compassion for others, improve dream recall.
- Orange sapphire or Padparadscha: stimulates the desire to speak to the world directly from one's heart. It combines creativity and spirituality: it is no coincidence that it is a useful talisman for artists, writers and singers.
- Pink Sapphire: Nurtures the wisdom of resilience. Stimulates emotions and promotes love, forgiveness and forgetting the past. Increase acceptance and strength of feelings.
- Violet Sapphire: Strengthens the wisdom of spiritual awakening. Stimulates meditation, vibrates with the

crown chakra and allows the Kundalini to rise unhindered. Promotes unity and peace.
- White Sapphire: brings wisdom and fortitude, helping to find within oneself the best solution to overcome the difficult obstacles encountered on one's spiritual journey. It gives the mind great clarity and improves communication with the Higher Self.
- Yellow Sapphire: brings wisdom and prosperity.
- Blue Sapphire: it is very useful for spiritual growth and for increasing self-discipline, especially in daily activities that require attention. Furthermore, it gives a lot of professional support, stimulates ingenuity and wisdom and increases common sense in carrying out one's profession. It is a stone symbol of integrity, so it is very effective for the quick and positive resolution of legal issues or in some way related to justice. Blue sapphire, again, is a stone of love, commitment and fidelity, so much so that it can be used in engagement rings.

Sapphire is great for calming the mind, aiding in the release of tension from unwanted thoughts; encourages intuition, bringing lightness, joy and balance.

The Stones of the Zodiac

The correspondences that exist between men and stones have been highlighted in past centuries in the so-called "stone books" (Lithica), including the one compiled by Theophrastus, Greek philosopher, pupil and successor of Aristotle.

The Zodiac, a word of Greek origin, means "way of animals", even if our Zodiac, unlike the Chinese one, contains three human images: a woman (Virgo), a man (Aquarius) and two children (Gemini).

It is made up of twelve constellations arranged like a circle along the celestial road traveled by the Sun in its apparent motion around the Earth. This course of the Sun is divided into the well-known 12 signs.

In the 4th century BC, when the foundations of the Greek astronomical school were laid, the Sun crossed the constellations of the zodiac starting from that of Aries where it was during the vernal equinox, remaining about a month in each constellation. As a result of the precession of the equinoxes, on March 21, the vernal equinox, the sun is currently no longer in the constellation of Aries, but in the previous one of Pisces, since in the last 2,300 years the constellations have moved by an entire constellation towards West. This process repeats itself every 25,595 years.

To preserve, therefore, the use of the ancient succession of zodiacal constellations, the so-called "signs of the Zodiac" were introduced to which the same names as the zodiacal constellations were given.

The shift between signs and constellations will always increase until they coincide again.

The Zodiac is also divided by elements: fire, earth, water, air and the planetary influence has been associated with gems:

- Fiery Ruby represents the fire element

Fire attributes heat, vitality, energy, combativeness, paternalism, desire to protect the weak but also to dominate them, generosity, healthy appetites of all kinds.
Aries, Leo, Sagittarius belong to it.

- The Emerald represents the earth and its vegetation

The earth attributes stability, rationality, love for traditions, desire for material possessions, need for essential relationships, simplicity of life, stability, continuity, lack of combativeness.
They include Taurus, Virgo, Capricorn.

- The Diamond represents the purity of water

Water attributes psychic restlessness, depth of feelings and passions, depth of thought, confidentiality, attraction to complicated situations, need to test oneself, creativity, unstable relationships with things and people.
Cancer, Scorpio, Pisces belong to it.

- Sapphire blue represents air

Air attributes intelligence, creativity, love of beauty, little sense of tradition, mental independence, irony, mobility, mental restlessness, ability to turn the page, pacifism. This includes Gemini, Libra, Aquarius.

Furthermore, the signs of the Zodiac can be divided into four groups characterized by various mythological periods and psychological correspondences.

The first three groups correspond to the three generations of gods: Uranus, Cronos and Zeus and to the three levels of development of consciousness: the unconscious, the conscious and the superconscious.

- The first group includes Pisces - Aries - Taurus and corresponds to the mythological period of Uranus, a period in which cosmic energies express themselves, in relation to man, instinctively, giving great space to the unconscious, impulsivity and imagination . It is a period characterized by such an uncontrolled proliferation of force that, sometimes, it ends up destroying even what it generates.

- The second group, made up of Gemini - Cancer - Leo, corresponds to the mythological period of Cronos, son of Uranus, who put an end to the first generation of the gods by making his father Uranus sterile and devouring his own children with the exception of Zeus, saved by his mother by clever deception. It is time for discernment and analysis in which the need for fine-tuning is felt: awareness of the self is born.

- The third group includes Virgo - Libra - Scorpio and corresponds to the mythological period of Zeus. This period marks an organized and orderly new beginning. The kingdom of Zeus is the kingdom of the spirit, it is the moment in which man becomes clearly aware of himself.

- The fourth group is formed by Sagittarius Capricorn - Aquarius.

Aries

Aries is the first sign of the zodiac, known for its fiery and energetic personality. People born under this sign are sincere, passionate, stubborn and optimistic. They are often people who tend to look first at themselves before others and are also protagonists in the actions of a group. A flaw of this zodiac sign is that he is very good at starting out, but he only finds it difficult to complete things, because he always gets carried away by new ideas. He can't say no to something new to throw himself into. However, he proves to be an excellent leader.

- Carnelian

Not only will it help you recharge your batteries, but it will also cure your (sometimes dangerous) impulsiveness. Furthermore, this stone infuses vitality, optimism, happiness and helps eliminate negative feelings such as jealousy and envy, improving mood. Amethyst is suitable as a complementary stone for those born under this sign.

- Red coral

Red coral is not really a stone but a limestone skeleton. A symbol of protection par excellence and, in the case of those born under the sign of Aries, this aspect is further strengthened. Helps keep the evil eye away.
Red coral is actually also known to energize and prevent emotional imbalances, especially those that lead to negative behaviors and self-saboteurs.

- Ruby

The ruby for the Indians of America is the lucky stone par excellence. A talisman of passion and prosperity, considered by the ancients to be even more precious than a diamond. It is an important symbol and evokes sexuality but also spiritual love.

- Red Jasper

Jasper gives courage and prosperity, and helps to rebel against the attempts of submission by others. Native Americans considered it the Blood of the Earth. This quartz increases physical but also mental resistance, thanks to it you learn to externalize problems and ask for help when you need it.

- Carnelian

Carnelian is a protective stone against negative energies and also against diseases. It teaches how to live in a more harmonious relationship with others. It is a very positive stone to give to an unborn child because it wishes a life of prosperity and abundance.

- Garnet

Garnet brings light to even the darkest situations. This stone for Aries is perfect if they have lost their usual optimism and desire to take on exciting new challenges.

Taurus

Ruled by Venus, Taurus appreciates the finer things in life, especially love. He has a great artistic sense and does not like to leave his destiny at the mercy of events. Except for situations of great discomfort, he takes matters into his own hands and from a dark period manages to get out of trouble on his own.
Those born under the sign of Taurus are stubborn people. They take a stand and keep going until they have achieved victory. From the outside they are often judged as materialistic but in reality, it is not at all uncommon for them to yearn for love. They are sentimentalists and very loyal in love, as well as in friendship. They fight for what they want, both privately and professionally.

- Rose Quartz

Rose Quartz can help this sign open the heart chakra and release a healthy dose of romance.
But not only that, always carrying a small rose quartz with you can help protect it from future potential heart breaks.

- Green Jade

Green jade is one of the best-known stones in crystallotherapy; it is a symbol of material and spiritual wealth. It is said to protect against negative energies. It is particularly loved both as a protective and ornamental stone, on the market you can find beautiful ones but you have to be careful of imitations.

- Green Tourmaline

Green tourmaline in dark times helps us recognize the positive aspects of life and appreciate them more. Increase the positive vibes of our surroundings.

- Green Aventurine

Green aventurine is a perfect stone for Taurus in search of lost inspiration, just the one needed to reach the end of a path. It also promotes the desire to compare oneself with others.
It is one of the easiest stones to find, but one must always be careful of its authenticity.

- Green Fluorite

Green Fluorite helps to break free from both physical and emotional addictions. With green fluorite you get to find the balance between mind and heart.

Gemini

People born under the sign of Gemini are particularly prone to interpersonal relationships. They are intelligent people, love to party and bring joy to the group thanks to their lively imagination. They are capable of understanding well two very different points of view, which is why they are unlikely to be able to take sides on one side or the other. An aspect that sometimes people don't like very much.
Some Geminis are moody. They change mood constantly and don't have a strong character. They tend to follow the others, adapting to the most diverse situations. They are people with many interests but, if they are not careful in choosing one, they risk not being able to make them something more than simple hobbies. They are curious, smart people, they love being in company and they are sincere people in relationships.

- Citrine Quartz

Citrine Quartz positively influences ideas and intelligence, and is definitely perfect for Gemini.
The use of this crystal will also help the sign improve their memory and have more mental energy. To be used absolutely when you have to study for an important exam.
Citrine quartz, solar stone par excellence, perhaps the best known of the yellow stones. It helps transform ideas and projects that are still in your mind for now into useful and productive actions. Not only that, it is considered a stone capable of attracting wealth into the wearer's life

- Topaz

Topaz is a symbol of courage and wisdom. It is a stone used in crystal therapy. Just like those born under the zodiac sign of

Gemini, wherever it is it brings good mood. It teaches you to assert your authority.

- Agate

Agate is a naturally occurring stone of many colors. Among its advantages is that it gives a lot of optimism and energy, both physical and mental. It helps, among other things, to perceive more clearly what are true desires rather than just passing ones.

Cancer

The sign of Cancer is governed by the element of water.
He loves to protect what belongs to him, especially the intimacy of the spaces to which he is strongly attached. He feels strongly the values of home and family, in which he seeks refuge to protect himself from the dangers of the environment. In negative times he can notice the risk in everything, to the point of isolating himself as a defense weapon.
In his environments and in his soul he allows only very few people to enter, those he really deems worthy of trust. For those unfamiliar with the Cancer person, he may seem grumpy and unwilling to be affectionate; in reality, to the people who are close to her show all your affection. He is endowed with great sensitivity, is kind and is careful not to offend others.

- Moonstone

You know, on a bad day, sweet Cancer can experience super intense emotions that can bring out anxieties and paranoia. The Moonstone is, in this respect, the ideal crystal for this water sign. In fact, its power is to relieve inner tensions, giving vibes of calm and serenity, and even help stabilize their sometimes fluctuating and dramatic sensations.
The moonstone acts on the entire female reproductive system. It balances the body's energies better than any other stone and for this reason it is advisable to use it if in this period you feel you are experiencing a profound imbalance. Among other beneficial effects there is one that strengthens the personality.

- Pearl

The pearl stabilizes the wearer's mood. Help release emotions, accepting other people's love without needing to have continuous demonstrations. Giving someone a pearl is certainly a beautiful gesture, considering its economic value. For a person born under the sign of Cancer it is even more suitable.

- Rock Crystal

Rock crystal promotes sincerity. Bring joy and serenity in the darkest moments. It makes the passage of energy more fluid and in crystallotherapy it is used above all for this reason.

- Ruby

Ruby was once believed to make anyone wearing it invulnerable. Today, however, it is used when we feel a little lazy and we seem to no longer be able to feel external stimuli. Often it is a block related to the first chakra.

- Emerald

The emerald is in tune with the soul of Cancer because it is considered a stone of love and friendship, in their pure and selfless version. Basically, however, it can be used simply to restore well-being in one's life and to feel in tune with others and with the whole universe.

Leo

The sign of Leo is ruled by the element of fire and the ruling planet is the sun. Those born under this sign have a strong character, are vital and outgoing.
He often sees the whole existence, even from the point of view of the smallest challenge, a struggle for survival, to emerge and never to be overwhelmed by others. He tends to dominate and often comes to feel master of the world, the center of attention; in reality, however, despite the fact that he hardly realizes this, it is really easy to deceive him, and this is because, being a little vain, he believes all flattery. Which is even easier because of his generosity and kindness.
It is rare for someone born under the sign of Leo to show their suffering in public. It's much easier for you to silently endure until the pain is over.

- Eye of the Tiger

The Tiger's Eye is known as the traditional crystal of Leo, because it allows you to channel greater creativity and positivity towards the sign. This amber-colored stone is capable of harmonizing the energy centers, allowing you to reach new positivity and a new balance more easily and with protection.

- Diamond

In crystallotherapy the diamond is widely used because it gives vitality, regenerates and purifies; it helps to overcome fear but also any depressive states. It helps to learn new concepts, therefore suitable for those who are facing a period of training and learning.

- Amber

Connected to both the element of fire and that of ether, of energy, it enhances the solar nature of this zodiac sign. It is the stone of spontaneity, optimism and openness towards others. It gives creativity and helps to achieve success. You can opt for a beautiful amber stone to always carry with you.

- Citrine Quartz

The openness of mind that citrine offers is useful to Leo because it helps him recognize those flattery made with the sole purpose of manipulating him.

Virgo

Virgo people have a sense of duty and always remain very humble. They never sit too long without doing anything, they want to feel useful and sitting still for them is synonymous with wasted time. The tendency to perfectionism, however, can prevent him from seeing the whole, for this reason his most frequent mistake is to launch himself into projects where he is not clear what the result is. Sometimes character leads to selfishness, to being critical. Among the various defects we also find hypochondria, often those born under the sign of Virgo fall into this trap.

- Red Jasper

Virgo and Red Jasper have a lot in common: both are known to bring practicality and clarity to any sphere. For this reason it is definitely the perfect crystal for this earth sign.
Red Jasper gives Virgo a greater attention span, already hyper-organized and analytical than her, allowing all problems to be resolved quickly and smoothly.

- Sapphire

Sapphire commands the water element, represents truth and constancy. It also helps strengthen mutual understanding, as well as loyalty. It has a calming effect and reduces anxiety, typical of those born under the sign of Virgo.

- Carnelian

Carnelian gives vitality and drives away negative feelings. Very useful for improving interpersonal relationships.
For those born under the sign of Virgo, carnelian is of great help, it teaches us to take many things a little more lightly to better enjoy the moment.

- Amethyst

Amethyst brings serenity and balance to life. He drives away states of agitation, especially those due to the launch of a new project. It should be used to see a situation not in detail but from above, in a generic way.

- Rose Quartz

Considered the stone of love, it helps to overcome emotional and sentimental wounds and to open up more to people to show them how you feel.

Libra

People born under the sign of Libra tend to be very altruistic, tend to strengthen relationships with others at every opportunity and are always willing to work together to achieve goals. They are well inclined to married life, especially the balanced one without too many jolts. They are reliable in love and manage to bring peace of mind.
It is a zodiac sign that tends towards objectivity, defends justice, always tries to reduce conflicts and does not like to foment them, for this reason "everything is fine for him" in order to avoid confrontation.

- Lapis lazuli

Its intense blue color recalls that of the sky and the gold veins the stars, a perfect pattern for that Libra aesthete. Lapis Lazuli helps balance inner energies which is why it pairs so well with this air sign.
The blue crystal encourages the sign to be more self-aware and helps them to accept themselves for who they are, rediscovering their personal harmony.

- Rose Quartz

Rose Quartz fits perfectly with the calm and balanced nature of those born under the sign of Libra. Basically it is ideal to wear it as a necklace to reduce anxiety and stress. It is your ideal lucky charm if you wish to discover your hidden gifts and talents. There are many rose quartz necklaces to choose from but if you want, you can also opt for rings, bracelets and earrings.

- Green tourmaline

It helps to highlight the most positive events of every single day, thus learning to welcome the good. Reduces tiredness and helps you stay focused on your goals. Green tourmaline is a fairly rare stone and therefore expensive, certainly however, especially if you want to make a unique gift to a loved one born under the sign of Libra, this is the perfect stone.

- Opal

The opal is a beautiful lucky stone, it stimulates, in fact, the desire for change already present in all people. Suitable for those who want to be more optimistic about their future. It helps transform negative feelings into positive ones.

- Malachite

Malachite is a green stone particularly appreciated for the various shades and round shapes it creates. On an energy level it is considered a good lucky charm for those born under the sign of Libra because it makes them more aware of their emotions, of past traumas, of what it is now time to let go because it only hurts.
Thanks to her then it is possible to learn to manage fear.

- Chrysoprase

Chrysoprase is a stone indicated for people who wish to let go of fears and want to overcome any form of addiction, both physical and mental. It helps to see life more positively, to become less obsessed with issues.

Scorpio

Among the 12 signs of the zodiac, Scorpio is, perhaps, the most profound.
He thinks about what he is told and does not take others' ideas lightly; when he feels attacked, however, he reacts immediately and goes on the attack. Sometimes with right reasons, other times a little too much when considering the slightest wrong.
Scorpio is intelligent and just can't tolerate being around people who aren't. Sensual and passionate, he doesn't even like frivolous relationships. He always looks for a reason behind every story of love or friendship.

- Obsidian

It is a powerful talisman with protective power.
Always carrying this stone with you will allow you to make great personal changes in a short time, working on your hidden problems that can generate suffering.
It helps protect against negative vibes and enhance the intuitive side of this water sign. Finally, Obsidian pushes you to face your own shadows, bringing to light all those situations that do not yet have a solution.

- Ruby

Considered a noble stone, ruby sharpens the mind. Gives courage, greater self-esteem and great concentration on everything you do. To be used in the dark moments of life.

- Carnelian

Optimism, cheerfulness and maximum concentration on the present.
Carnelian can be of great help to Scorpio, especially if he wants to mitigate his tendency to get on tenterhooks right away.

- Red jasper

Also known as the warrior stone, jasper promotes both action and courage. Useful to increase the spirit of initiative and honesty. Fight guilt.

- Fire opal

Lucky stone for Scorpio if he is faced with a fresh start. It highlights his fiery spirit and passion.

Sagittarius

Those born under the sign of Sagittarius can hardly sit still; they need to practice sports, to keep their mind trained and to intervene immediately when a problem arises, however at the risk of being a little impulsive in choosing the solution. They love adventure and in everything they do they tend to be very optimistic and passionate.
For this reason they manage in most cases to achieve their goals, often also bringing home excellent results. They are hardly let down by a defeat; instead, they are ready to get up again and concentrate, give their all to get exactly where they want.
A temperament also due to its dominant element, fire, full of passion and warmth. It illuminates, sees beyond the dark, knows how to convey passions and ideals.
But occasionally his inability to stop and think before acting can burn him out. When he gets angry he does it in a devastating way.

- Turquoise

This stone gives greater balance between emotions and feelings, helps manage the stress of "too many things to do" (typical attitude of the sign) and teaches to recognize and prioritize the most useful projects for one's well-being.

- Azurite

It makes a little more critical, in this way it helps to better classify the choices and make the most sensible decisions. It makes communication more fluid.

- Topaz

Topaz strengthens those abilities already innate in the Sagittarius personality, namely being positive, getting up after a fall and seeing beyond the dark period that one is facing.

- Zircon

It helps to get rid of the attachment of material things and appreciate more the spiritual side of life. It allows you to get back in touch with your roots.

Capricorn

The person born under the sign of Capricorn is by nature shy, hardly bonds with people but when he does he is always present, available and transforms into one of the most affectionate people there is.
Capricorn is a very good friend, he takes care of his health, he is careful not to fall into "sick" relationships. Before taking a step, he always takes into account all the pros and cons.

- Jade

Precious stone with an intense green color; its power is to strengthen memory and promote communication, courage and thought.
In short, it can help the sign to say aloud what it needs, without hesitation. Jade will help the sign to manifest its truest and deepest desires, especially in the relational and work sphere.

- Black Onyx

The birthstone par excellence is the black onyx, a truly beautiful chalcedony.
With black onyx you can sleep peaceful dreams, or almost.
Basically, this stone absorbs negative energies to transform them into positive energies. In the past it was used against the evil eye.

- Black Tourmaline

Black tourmaline is another stone that purifies energies. It helps to recognize your mistakes and learn from them for the future. Wearing black tourmaline helps shield yourself from negativity.

- Black Obsidian

It brings to light the negative aspects of the personality to work with, without creating an immediate upheaval. It allows you to do a gradual work on yourself. It is also known as the shamanic stone, as it was used to address physical problems and help the person heal.

- Smoky Quartz

Helps manage fear and stress. Strengthens contact with higher energies and allows you to do deep introspective work. It is a very strong energy stone.

It is a stone which, among other things, as well as working as a lucky charm for those born under the sign of Capricorn, allows you to keep electromagnetic waves away.

Acquarius

The purpose of life of people born under the sign of Aquarius seems to have to improve everyone's life: they sacrifice themselves for their colleagues, for their boyfriend, for their parents.
However, they do not show excessive attachment and, on the contrary, they appear very detached in social and impersonal relationships.
They strongly believe in justice and are people with strong ideals. However, they tend to change their minds and plans often. This is because they need continuous stimuli, they love the freedom of being able to make their own decisions independently without having to account to anyone.

- Aquamarine

This stone works on the mental plane, helping the Aquarius sign to speed up reasoning processes and quickly find the solution to every question. Furthermore, it is also particularly suitable for working on your emotions, especially when you have blocks and difficulties in letting go with others.

- Rock Crystal

If Aquarius as a sign is often unbalanced in choices and feelings, rock crystal is perfect precisely because it brings emotional stability. On the other hand, however, it enhances the desire for solitude as it is a crystal that promotes introspection.

- Blue sapphire

A blue sapphire necklace has its price and certainly isn't the right gift for any occasion. However if you like gemstones, it can be a good idea. It brings order among thoughts and gives will to achieve the goals set.

- Turquoise

A turquoise pendant is certainly an appreciated gift. It brings balance to feelings, it helps you forgive yourself and others for any past mistakes (also because those who don't commit them). Strengthens the qualities of the sign, individuality, but for the common good.

Pisces

People born under the sign of Pisces are often described as kind-hearted, open-minded and calm.
They are, however, very prone to blame for those negative experiences that life throws at them; despite this, their positive aspects are not dulled and they manage to inspire other people. They are sensitive, empathetic and in life can find their outlet in the artistic sector.
Those born under the rule of Pisces have a good heart, in fact, they willingly lend themselves to helping others without expecting anything in return. Negative experiences put them to the test and they are tempted by addictions. He has introverted traits, they can be fearful and pour out fears towards those they love. They idealize love and this leads them to burning burns. They live each of their relationships with passion and maximum involvement.

- Amethyst

This purple stone represents spiritual wisdom, a typical characteristic of this water sign.
Not only that, Amethyst can also help strengthen intuition and protect against negative vibes, which is perfect for more sensitive Pisces. Finally, the use of this crystal can bring greater concentration, improving the ability to pay attention to everything that is important and to bring Pisces down to earth, always with his head in the clouds.

- Aquamarine

It helps to work a lot on emotions. It makes you more aware and is suitable for people with a calm character. Aquamarine is not an easy stone to find, working with it or wearing it as a lucky stone is undoubtedly a great experience. Its positive vibes help to find the right ideas first.

- Amazonite

Amazonite helps to overcome life's disappointments and traumas. It gives much more self-confidence and teaches you to say no from time to time, without giving more than you actually can.
Precisely for this reason it is suitable for those born under the sign of Pisces.

www.ingramcontent.com/pod-product-compliance
Lightning Source LLC
Chambersburg PA
CBHW071511040426
42444CB00008B/1598